DATE DUE

Se 28 '89	DEC 1 1 1991	DEC 2 9 2000
NOV 1 8 1988	FEB 1 7 1992	MAY 2 9 2000
De 17 '80	AUG 1 5 1992	JUN 2 3 2000
My 27 '89	NOV 1 2 1992	FEB 1 7 2003
Ju 17 '89	FEB 1 1 1993	DEC - 4 2004
AUG 3 1989	MAR 2 3 1993	APR 1 9 2005
Se 9 '89	MAR 2 6 1993	JAN 0 8 2008
Oc 28 '89	DEC 1 4 1993	FEB 2 3 2008
De 16 '89	OCT 2 7 1994	DEC - 8 2008
Fe 10 90	NOV 1 5 1994	MAY 0 9 2009
Mr 3 90	JUN 3 0 1995	
OCT 1 1 199	OCT 1 7 1996	OCT 1 6 2010
De 22 '90	OCT - 1 1998	JAN 1 3 2012
JAN 1 2 1991	JAN 2 7 2000	NOV 0 9 2013
MAR 6 1991	FEB - 7 2000	
AUG 1 2 1991	JUN 1 9 2000	
OCT 1 5 199	NOV 2 9 2000	

CARR McLEAN, TORONTO FORM #38-297

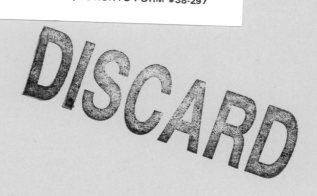

DISCARD

150 YEARS OF
CANADIAN
RAILROADS

150 YEARS OF
CANADIAN RAILROADS

Royce
PUBLICATIONS

Copyright © 1984
Winchmore Publishing
Services Limited

First published in Canada by
Royce Publications
Toronto, Canada

This edition was
produced by
Winchmore Publishing
Services Limited
40 Triton Square
London NW1 3HG

Printed in Yugoslavia

ISBN: 0-7740-3536-6

Contents

1 The Colonial System   7
2 The Pacific Railway   29
3 The National System   65
4 The Northern Lines   95
5 Resources Railways   117
6 Passenger Transport   129

CHAPTER ONE

THE COLONIAL SYSTEM

From the start of European exploration, the abundant natural waterways of Canada were the principal transportation routes, and for two centuries settlement was confined to the coasts and river banks. By the end of the 18th century the total population of the various colonies of British North America was perhaps 350,000, of whom about 20,000 were on the island of Newfoundland, which would remain independent of the mainland for another 150 years. Of the remainder, some 85,000 were settled in the maritime provinces of Nova Scotia and New Brunswick, while approximately 200,000 were the predominantly French-speaking inhabitants of Lower Canada, which extended along the banks of the St Lawrence as far as the Ottawa River on the north side and the United States border on the south; only 60,000 or so lived west of the Ottawa in the colony of Upper Canada. Beyond Lake Superior was a wilderness, traversed only by Indians and the fur traders of the Hudson's Bay Company and its new Montreal-based rival, the North West Company.

Within 30 years the population had trebled, and the most significant change was the steadily increasing proportion living in Upper Canada. Already Montreal, at the head of navigable water on the St Lawrence, with the Lachine rapids immediately upstream and the confluence of the Ottawa just beyond, was emerging as the principal trading centre: across the Ottawa the number of settlers now exceeded 200,000, still outnumbered by more than half a million Lower Canadians but now constituting a fifth of the colonies' total population. West of Montreal, however, communications were still inadequate. A good road system followed the thickly populated downstream banks of the St Lawrence, but in Upper Canada rivers and lakes were almost the only arteries of trade.

At the beginning of the 19th century there was an established network of water routes spreading westward from Montreal. The Ottawa river was the start of one, leading via Lake Nipissing and French River to Georgian Bay and the Great Lakes. Further up the St Lawrence, Lake Ontario was the focus of a series of routes leading north from the village of York – later renamed Toronto – to Georgian Bay by way of Lake Simcoe, or round the Niagara Falls to Lake Erie and beyond. All

Previous page: The locomotive *Dorchester* hauls the inaugural train on the Champlain and St Lawrence Railway between St John's and Laprairie, the first in Canada, on September 21, 1836.

Below: In the early nineteenth century waterways were the principal means of communication; the St Lawrence canal past the Lachine Rapids was opened in 1779, and is depicted here two years later.

these routes involved numerous portages, where boats and their loads had to be carried around rapids or across land breaks between the waterways, and before the War of 1812 there had been attempts to improve matters. A narrow canal past the Lachine rapids was completed in 1779 by military engineers, and in 1798 a canal past the Sault Ste Marie between Lakes Huron and Superior was built for the boats of the North West Company. Following the war, the fear of renewed hostilities provided the spur for further building: a new canal past the Lachine rapids was completed in 1825; the Welland Canal, by-passing the Niagara Falls, was opened in 1829; the construction of the Rideau Canal during the following decade provided a route via the Ottawa River to Lake Ontario; and by the 1840s further canals along the St Lawrence completed a navigable route all the way from Montreal to Lake Huron.

With all these improvements to the water routes there was a corresponding increase in the traffic they carried. Canoes were replaced by bigger boats and then by sailing schooners and steamships. At the same time, the volume of timber, furs and other exports was growing with the number of settlers, who in turn demanded greater quantities of supplies. But communications were still interrupted by frozen rivers for nearly half the year, resulting in highly unsatisfactory trading conditions.

An alternative route to the ocean, and the principal artery of communications with the northeastern United States, was provided by the Richelieu and Hudson Rivers, running north and south from Lake Champlain on the international border. The Hudson also formed an important part of one of the principal US routes to the west, especially after the Erie Canal, opened in 1825, connected its tributary, the Mohawk, with Lake Erie. Six years later an entirely new form of transport appeared in the form of the Mohawk and Hudson Railroad, opened in August 1831 to link Albany on the Hudson and Schenectady on the Mohawk. The success of the Mohawk and Hudson provoked a similar scheme to the north, and within six months royal assent had been given to a bill passed by the legislature of Lower Canada providing for the construction of a railway between Lake Champlain and the St Lawrence.

The significance of this route was the enormous reduction of the distance by water between Montreal and Lake Champlain, a total of a hundred miles down the St Lawrence to the junction with the Richelieu, and up the latter to St John's, at the head of the Richelieu rapids and the start of navigable water on the route south. By comparison, the distance between St John's and the nearest point on the St Lawrence – Laprairie, on the opposite bank from Montreal and only eight miles upstream – was a mere $14\frac{1}{2}$ miles. The intervening terrain, moreover, was virtually level: the ideal setting for a new railway.

Although the attractions of the scheme were obvious there was some difficulty in raising the necessary capital, and it was only at the instigation of a St John's merchant, Jason C. Pierce, that the Champlain and St Lawrence Railroad Company was finally set up in November 1834. Once under way, however, construction proceeded rapidly, on schedule and within the budget. By the end of 1835 the major construction works, including an embankment, a 400ft bridge over the Little River and the wharf for transshipment at Laprairie, were complete; the following spring saw the laying of the track well advanced and brought the launch of the ferry *Princess Victoria*, which would provide the link with Montreal itself; and in June the Stephenson locomotive *Dorchester* arrived at Montreal.

The official opening of the railway took place on July 21, 1836, when the *Dorchester*, with two coaches, and followed by others drawn by horses, proceeded from Laprairie to St John's, and after a celebratory banquet the locomotive with four coaches completed the return journey in just under an hour. The opening was misleading in one respect, however: the English locomotive proved as unsuitable for the first Canadian railway as its predecessors had on early American tracks, so that services (summer only for the time being) were operated by horse while the *Dorchester* was converted to a 4–2–0 configuration from its original 0–4–0, and two new locomotives were ordered from Norris of Philadelphia for the 1837 season.

Although the Champlain and St Lawrence was only one of a number of railways proposed during the 1830s, it was more than ten years before any new lines became operational. The Montreal and Lachine Railroad, running eight miles from Montreal to a wharf at the head of the rapids, and with five intermediate stops, was officially opened on November 19, 1847, though regular services did not begin until the following spring. In 1850 another short line was opened between the village of Industrie, now the industrial

town of Joliette, and the St Lawrence, and in 1854 the Carillon-Grenville section of the planned Montreal and Ottawa (originally Bytown) Railway began operations to connect with steam ship services to and from Montreal and Ottawa either side of an eleven-mile series of rapids on the Ottawa River.

Once again, however, new railroads south of the international border were to stimulate construction in Canada. In September 1850

Above: A model of the *Dorchester*, first locomotive on the Champlain and St Lawrence Railway, before its conversion to a more suitable 4–2–0 configuration.

St Lawrence and the Montreal Lachine responded to this threat with their own extensions, the former with a cut-off to Lambert, directly across the river from Montreal, at its northern end and an extension to Rouses Point in the south. The Montreal and Lachine, meanwhile, bought the Lake St Louis and Province Line Railway, which was planning a line from Caughnawaga, opposite Lachine, to the US border, merging with the latter company to form the New York and Montreal Railroad.

At the same time, the Montreal and Lachine incorporated another new company, the St Lawrence and Ottawa Grand Junction Railroad, to be built up the Ottawa valley to Grenville and south to Prescott, on the north shore of the St Lawrence opposite the Ogdensburgh terminus of the Northern Railroad. Then, rebuffed by the Northern in its quest for a junction, the Montreal and Lachine proprietors formed another new company, the Montreal and Plattsburgh, which would provide a connection via a car ferry on Lake Champlain with the Rutland and Burlington Railroad in Vermont.

The Ottawa and Prescott section of the St Lawrence and Ottawa Grand Junction was opened in December 1854, but within four years was in the hands of the receiver, to be revived in 1867 without the Grand Junction to its name; and even before it was opened the southern extensions of the two rivals were in trouble. The Champlain and St Lawrence's extension to Rouses Point was opened in August 1851, and the St Lambert cut-off in January 1852, to be joined by the Montreal and New York in September of that year, but the costs of construction had crippled the hitherto prosperous Champlain and St Lawrence, while the Montreal and Lachine had been hard up from the start, and the subsequent competition for the Lake Champlain traffic was too much: in 1857 the two railways merged to form the Montreal and Champlain Railroad.

At the same time as these pioneer enterprises were struggling to make the transition from simple portage railways to international freight carriers, a number of much more ambitious projects were under way. In 1849 the Provincial government passed an act empowering the government to guarantee the interest on loans raised for railway construction by companies owning at least 75 miles of railway, and one of the first to benefit was the St Lawrence and Atlantic. Originally proposed some years earlier, and subse-

the Northern Railroad was opened between Ogdensburgh, on the St Lawrence, and Rouses Point, on Lake Champlain, threatening to bypass Montreal and its fledgling railways altogether. Both the Champlain and

quently sustained, by John A. Poor, this venture and its twin, the Atlantic and St Lawrence, were designed to link Portland, on the Atlantic coast of Maine, and Montreal, the two companies forming, respectively, the Canadian and US parts of the route. Such a line had been made possible by the final establishment of the international border with Maine in 1842 and an agreement with the United States to allow duty-free trans-shipment of Canadian merchandise in 1846, but by February 1849, with the US section in difficulties and the first 30 miles of the Canadian portion from Longeuil complete, the company ran out of money, and it was only with government help that the line was completed in July 1854.

The main purpose of the guarantee act was to finance a railway link between the two Canadas and the maritime provinces of Nova Scotia and New Brunswick: Poor had his own ideas for the route, incorporating the European and North American Railway in 1850 to construct a line from Portland to Saint John, New Brunswick, and Halifax, Nova Scotia. This project, however, was overshadowed by various proposals for an alternative line north of the international boundary from the Atlantic to Quebec, Montreal and the Great Lakes, and the ultimate extent of the European and North American was a line from Saint John to Shediac, on the northern coast of New Brunswick, completed in 1860. Two years earlier another line be-

tween Halifax and Truro, with a branch to Windsor, had been completed under the auspices of the government of Nova Scotia, but it was to be another 16 years before the maritime provinces would achieve their rail link with the interior.

In the meantime, the guarantee act had come to the aid of another struggling enterprise. The Great Western Railway had been incorporated in 1845 to build across Canada West from Niagara Falls to Windsor, in the hope of attracting American traffic between the Erie canal and the Midwest; the scheme was subsequently altered to include a branch to Sarnia. Work on this trunk line was started in 1849, by January 1855 it was complete, and two months later the Niagara Falls

Above: The Honourable John Ross, first president of the British-backed Grand Trunk Railway of Canada, which was chartered in 1852 as part of the projected 'Main Line' between the Great Lakes and the maritime provinces.

Right: Officials and staff of the Grand Trunk Railway pose with the coal-fired locomotive No 377.

Inset: Passenger trains no longer stop at Grafton on the old Grank Trunk main line between Toronto and Montreal as their predecessors did in 1858, two years after its opening.

suspension bridge was opened. The Great Western's ambitions regarding international traffic met with a number of obstacles, however. In 1851 an amendment to the railway legislation had stipulated that government aid would be extended only to lines built to the newly adopted provincial gauge of 5ft 6in, while the American lines had already accepted the standard gauge of 4ft 8½in, so the prospects for through traffic were prejudiced almost from the beginning. At the same time, a series of competing lines were already appearing.

In June 1858 the Buffalo and Lake Huron Railway was opened between Fort Erie, opposite Buffalo on the Niagara River, and Goderich, on Lake Huron, after prolonged difficulties. These included the destruction of sections of track by unpaid workers, and, more significantly, a battle for the right of way at Stratford with an even more formidable competitor in the shape of the Grand Trunk Railway.

This company had been formed by the Canadian politician Sir Francis Hincks and the English contractor William Jackson, and was chartered in November 1852 in two parts, the Grand Trunk Railways of Canada and of Canada East. The former was originally intended to run from Montreal via Kingston to

GRAND TRUNK RAILWAY.

(J.)
40.
No. 982
Good for   First Class,   Full Fares, $
"   Second "   1858.
"   Third "
                                              1858.
                lbs. Extra Baggage
TORONTO To
AMOUNT $ Agent.

Above: Nineteenth century scene at the former St Williams, Ontario, station of the Grand Trunk Railway.

Toronto, while the latter would be a 153-mile line along the south shore of the St Lawrence from Lévis, opposite Quebec City, to Trois Pistoles. In this form the Grand Trunk would form the central section of a projected 'main line', with the Great Western providing the link with the American Midwest, the Quebec and Richmond, incorporated in 1850 but still far from complete, linking the Grand Trunk East with the St Lawrence and Atlantic, and a new line east from Trois Pistoles to the maritime provinces to be built at a later date.

Within a couple of years, however, it had become a major system in its own right, leasing the St Lawrence and Atlantic/Atlantic and St Lawrence line to Portland along with the Quebec–Richmond connection, undertaking to bridge the St Lawrence at Montreal, and abandoning the connection with the Great Western in favour of its own line to Sarnia. Such an ambitious programme of construction was risky enough in itself, but in simultaneously acquiring the accumulated debts of the Portland lines and the Quebec connection the Grand Trunk was adding extra hurdles. Its difficulties were further compounded by political instability and

public prejudice, by the refusal of the English bankers who acted as financial agents to the Province of Canada to sell more than half the shares at the original flotation, and by the contractors' failure to reckon with the rigours of the Canadian winter.

Thus the company was in no position to withstand a series of major setbacks. The Atlantic and St Lawrence, in the first place, proved to be a travesty of a railway, requiring extensive rehabilitation without bringing in enough income to pay the interest on its debts; the original estimates for construction proved to be too low; and the outbreak of the Crimean War in the spring of 1854 brought massive inflation in its wake. Nevertheless, the contractors kept on building, and with the help of government finance the railway gradually took shape. The line between Lévis and Richmond was opened in November 1854, the Hamilton–Toronto section was completed in October 1855, a year before the first train ran over the completed line from Montreal to Toronto, and with the opening of the Victoria Bridge at the end of 1859 there were rails all the way from the Atlantic seaboard to Windsor.

By this stage the Grand Trunk and Great Western had already become rivals west of Toronto. Even before the line from Toronto to Sarnia was opened in July 1856 a 51-mile branch line from St Mary's to the south had been incorporated as the London and Grand Trunk Junction Railway, and two years later the Chicago, Detroit and Canada Grand Trunk Junction was under way between Port Huron, across the St Clair River from Sarnia, and Detroit. This move to increase traffic from the United States across Canada to Portland was obviously a threat to the Great Western, and an example of the extent of the rate-cutting that ensued is provided by the fact that during 1860 the Grand Trunk's rates on some produce between the Midwest and Liverpool, England, were lower than those of American lines for moving the same goods from Chicago to New York.

Despite its troubles, the Grand Trunk survived. A shareholders' revolt in 1861 resulted in the appointment of new management, and the Grand Trunk Arrangements Act of 1862 enabled the company to raise fresh capital, though it also stipulated that revenues should be applied to interest payments on outstanding debts and bonds. At the same time, competition in the Ontario peninsula intensified. The Erie and Niagara Railway, chartered in

Below: The St Lawrence River and the Grand Trunk Railway's Victoria Bridge at Montreal in 1859, the year in which the bridge was opened.

1869 and renamed the Canada Southern in the following year, was countered by the Great Western's Canada Air Line: the former ran from Fort Erie to Amerherstburg on the Detroit River, the latter from Glencoe in the west to Fort Erie, where both, along with the Grand Trunk's Buffalo and Lake Huron subsidiary, converged on the new International Bridge over the Niagara River, opened in October of that year. By this stage the requirement for the use of the provincial gauge had been repealed, and both the Grand Trunk and the Great Western had begun conversion to standard gauge, at the same time replacing old iron rails with steel.

The need to generate traffic had also forced both lines to begin acquiring the short lines that were appearing all over southern Ontario. The motives behind these lines were as various as the communities that had sponsored them. They were built because a town was on the route of one of the new trunk lines, or because it was being bypassed; to channel the produce of an inland area to a particular port, or in the hope of settling an uninhabited area; because no other local line existed, or to compete with one being built. Generally, however, it was the increasing surpluses of timber, corn or minerals being produced in the region, along with the growing volume of through traffic that encouraged dreams of railway-based prosperity.

The results of these schemes were equally varied. Some were soundly constructed along well-chosen routes, attracting profitable business and stimulating growth. Others, whether through unscrupulousness or incompetence, or as a result of the regular financial panics of the period, were never finished, or were so much more expensive than the estimates that they carried an insupportable burden of debt from the outset: where the debts could be disposed of, and where there was either potential profit or possible nuisance value either the Grand Trunk or the Great Western would eventually take an interest. And before the ultimate consolidation of the two trunk lines some substantial independent or quasi-independent groups appeared in the area.

Among the earliest charters in Upper Canada was that of the Cobourg Railroad, established in 1834, and finally built as the Cobourg and Peterborough Railway between the Lake Ontario port and the inland industrial centre in 1854. Never particularly successful, it added branches to the Marmora iron works and Chemong Lake before being absorbed by the Grand Trunk in 1893. A more substantial enterprise centred on Peterborough originated as the Peterborough and Port Hope at the end of 1846: completed as the Port Hope, Lindsay and Beaverton in 1858 it comprised a total of 55 miles, with a main line between Port Hope and Lindsay and a branch to Peterborough. Following a period of prosperity it became the Midland Railway of Canada at the end of 1869, adding a spur from Peterborough to Lakefield and an extension via Beaverton and Orillia to the port of Midland, on Georgian Bay, during the next decade.

During the 1870s the Midland took over a number of other short lines. Among these were the Grand Junction Railway, completed between Peterborough and Belleville in 1880; the Toronto and Nipissing, running 88 miles north from Scarborough to Coboconk, and originally a narrow-gauge line before its sale to the Midland in 1881; and the 55-mile Victoria Railway, running north from Lindsay via Fenelon Falls, its original destination, to Haliburton. The result was a 450-mile system, which in 1883 became part of the Grand Trunk complex, retaining its old name for another ten years.

The Great Western had also extended its network in the early 1870s. The acquisition of the unfinished Wellington, Grey and Bruce in 1869 resulted in the latter being completed from Guelph, on the Great Western main line, to Southampton, on Owen Sound, by the end of 1872, and another two years brought the opening of a branch to Kincardine. In 1873 the Great Western also leased the incomplete London, Huron and Bruce, and completed this line from a few miles west of London via Clinton to a junction with the Kincardine branch of the Wellington, Grey and Bruce. South of the original main line the London and Port Stanley Railway was leased in 1871, and the Brantford, Norfolk and Port Burwell was leased in 1877, an extension from its original terminus at Tillsonburg to a junction with the main line forming a convenient link with the Canada Air Line to the south.

Hardly had the Great Western completed these transactions than it was taken over itself. Sporadic rate agreements with the Grand Trunk had repeatedly given way to fresh bouts of rate-cutting, and even as it was expanding the company was suffering a series of setbacks in its traffic with the United States. The position improved during the second half of the decade, and prospects for the future looked good, but this very fact inspired the Grand Trunk to mount a takeover: ultimately, the terms offered to the Great Western's shareholders proved good enough to induce them to reject the advice of the board, and in August 1882 the two companies formally amalgamated.

Six years later the Grand Trunk acquired another group of railways in Ontario to complete an extensive system. The Northern Railway had originated as the Toronto, Simcoe and Lake Huron Union Railroad, incorporated in 1849 and intended to build from Toronto by way of Barrie, on the eastern arm of Lake Simcoe, to Georgian Bay. Although originally promoted by the town of Barrie, the line built in the early 1850s turned west at Allandale just short of Barrie, and headed for a point on the bay at the site of Collingwood. This was reached in 1855, by which time the name had been changed to Ontario, Simcoe and Huron Union, but within three years the railway was in such trouble that it was reorganised as the Northern Railway of Canada, and in 1859 its ownership was transferred temporarily to the Crown. With government assistance the company enjoyed relative prosperity during the 1860s, and in the 1870s it sponsored the North Grey Railway, from Collingwood to Meaford, 20 miles to the west, and the Toronto, Simcoe and Muskoka Junction, from Barrie to Gravenhurst, on Lake Muskoka, ultimately taking over these branches. The Northern also acquired the North Simcoe Railway, from a junction at Colwell to Penetanguishene, on Georgian Bay.

In the meantime, a series of lines had been planned from Hamilton without result until the Hamilton and North Western got under way in 1874. This line was opened to Barrie at the beginning of 1878, and a branch to Collingwood was completed a year later. Rather than engage in competition for the same traffic, the Northern and the Hamilton and North Western joined forces in a new company, the Northern and North Western, formed in 1879, and two years later another new company, the Northern, North Western and Sault Ste Marie, was incorporated to build north and west from Gravenhurst. Dominion subsidies and a change of name to Northern and Pacific Junction saw the line extended as far as Callander, to the east of Lake Nipissing, but in constructing this line the promoters had overextended their credit, paving the way for a takeover by the Grand Trunk. This was duly accomplished in January 1888.

Plush upholstery and ornate decoration in a late nineteenth-century sleeping car of the Grand Trunk. The berths were designed to be lowered from the ceiling.

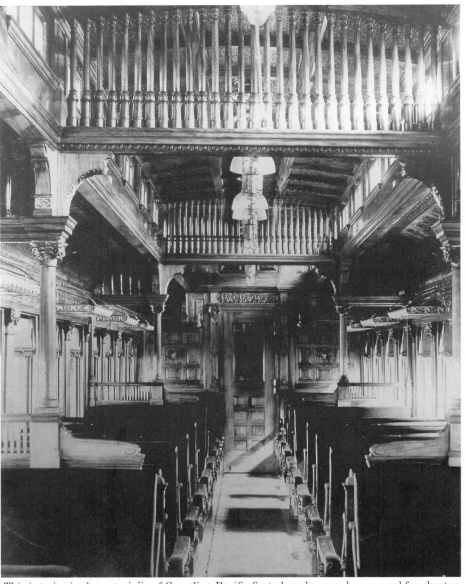

This interior is characteristic of Canadian Pacific first class day coaches as used for shorter journeys in eastern Canada toward the end of the century.

Below: A Canadian Pacific passenger train from Nakusp, British Columbia, arriving at Rosebery on Slocan lake and a rendezvous with the steamer *Slocan*.

The significance of the line to the north lay in an anticipated junction with the new Canadian Pacific Railway, one of the fruits of the Confederation which had been concluded in 1867 between the provinces of Nova

Sandford Fleming.

Scotia, New Brunswick, Quebec and Ontario to form the Dominion of Canada, and the subsequent addition of Manitoba, the North west Territories in 1870 and of British Columbia in 1871. The price of British Columbia's participation was the Pacific railway: the maritime provinces, similarly, had demanded their own rail link with the inland provinces.

One of the Grand Trunk's earliest commitments had been the line along the south shore of the St Lawrence to Trois Pistoles: in the event, this had reached no further than Rivière du Loup, 27 miles short of its original objective. Nor had the maritime provinces made any progress since the completion of the Nova Scotia Railway and the European and North American line from Saint John to Shediac. At the constitutional conferences that preceded federation, however, the Intercolonial Railway was a principal point of discussion, and the articles of federation included a specific undertaking to build the line.

The first step was to link the existing Nova Scotia and New Brunswick lines, but in the meantime the Nova Scotia government undertook to build an extension from Truro to Pictou. The work was carried out by Sandford Fleming, who had earlier served as Chief Engineer of the Northern Railway, before undertaking the first survey for the Intercolonial and becoming Chief Engineer of the

Left: The heavily decorated Ocean to Ocean special, first train to arrive at the Canadian Pacific's new Vancouver terminus on May 28, 1887.

25

Nova Scotia Railway, and was completed by May 1867, whereupon Fleming was free to take on a similar appointment with the Intercolonial itself. A route for the railway, based on Fleming's earlier surveys, ran north from Moncton to Bathurst, on Chaleur Bay, then northwest along the Matapedia River valley to the St Lawrence and southwest to a junction with the Grand Trunk at Rivière du Loup.

The work was overseen by a board of four railway commissioners, whose interference in the management and construction of the line was so counter-productive that, with the intervention of local politics and vested interests, the connecting line between Truro and Painsec Junction alone took until November 1872, at which point the existing lines

in Nova Scotia and New Brunswick were added to the Intercolonial. It was not until June 1876 that the complete line between Halifax and Rivière du Loup was ready for traffic. Even before this date the reputation of the line was so low that in April 1874 the railway commissioners were relieved of their responsibility for the Intercolonial, which was placed under the control of the Department of Public Works.

Before the year was out the Department of Public Works had another railway to administer, and the Dominion of Canada had another province. Prince Edward Island had declined to join in the original Confederation, and had made no attempt to build railways. In April 1871, however, perhaps under the influence of developments across the North-

umberland Strait, the provincial government passed an act covering the construction of a railway from end to end of the island, and their haste was such that within six months building had started.

Enthusiasm waned as quickly as it had grown. The prices fixed for the narrow-gauge line were so modest, and the contractors employed so inexperienced, that by the end of 1872 the island's government was petitioning the Dominion for membership on condition that the latter take over the railway. This was agreed, though the line that had been built was found to be in such a poor state that it was only after considerable argument that the Dominion government agreed to take it over.

Another commitment made by the Domin-ion government was the provision of a connection with the mainland. This was finally achieved by branch lines to Port Borden on the island and to Cape Tormentine on the mainland of New Brunswick with the nine-mile gap bridged by a car ferry. Even so, conditions in winter were so bad that it was nearly 20 years after the terminals were opened, in 1885, before a year-round service could be maintained.

Thus the railways had brought New Brunswick, Nova Scotia and Prince Edward Island into the Confederation, but there still remained the problem of building the promised line to the Pacific: without it not only British Columbia but the whole of the Canadian west might be lost to Californian gold prospectors and the farmers of the American Midwest.

Above: This 4–4–0 was the first locomotive to be produced by the Intercolonial Railway's own shops at Moncton in 1876.

CHAPTER TWO

THE PACIFIC RAILWAY

Previous page: The Dominion, Canadian Pacific's transcontinental train, headed by a Selkirk 2–10–4 alongside the Bow River in the Rocky Mountains.

Right: A relatively easy stretch of the Canadian Pacific's route through the Rockies: one of the crews employed by contractor Andrew Onderdonk in the lower Fraser Valley, 1883.

In 1846 the 49th parallel was established as the boundary between the United States and British North America west of Lake of the Woods. In 1849 Vancouver's Island, where the Hudson's Bay Company had established a Pacific coast headquarters at Fort Victoria in 1843, was granted to the company, but settlement was minimal until the discovery of gold on the Fraser River in 1856 brought a flood of prospectors, principally from California. James Douglas, combining the roles of Chief Factor for the company and Colonial Governor of the island, extended his control to the mainland until 1858, when Vancouver Island and British Columbia became separate colonies. The two were reunited in 1866, and in 1869 the Hudson's Bay Company reached a settlement with the Canadian and British governments whereby it surrendered its title to Rupert's Land, the old Red River settlement forming the basis for the new province of Manitoba and the remainder being administered by the Dominion. Finally, in July 1871 British Columbia, severely depressed in the aftermath of the gold rush, joined the Confederation.

The price of British Columbia's accession was the promise by Canadian prime minister Sir John A. Macdonald to start a railway to the Pacific within two years, and to complete it within ten. There was little point in British Columbia becoming a part of Canada without such an overland link – during the gold rush the sea journey round Cape Horn was a more practical proposition than the trek across the continent – but the same physical obstacles that lay in the path of the westward traveler would have to be overcome by a railway. The first requirement, then, was for a survey of possible routes: Sandford Fleming was given the job, on top of his Intercolonial responsibilities, and with 800 men at his disposal the work was started on July 20, 1871, the date of British Columbia's admission to the Confederation.

Fleming divided the terrain to be surveyed into three; the Woodland division north of the Great Lakes, the Mountain division in the west and the Prairie division between. The successive ranges of mountains parallel to the Pacific coast were the most obvious barrier: the first crossing had been made by Alexander Mackenzie in 1893, by way of the Peace River to the ocean at Dean Channel, and in 1808 Simon Fraser had descended the river named after him from Prince George to its mouth. But neither route offered a practical means of access, and during the gold

rush of the 1850s, when the estuary of the Fraser had been established as the sole point of entry to British Columbia, it had been necessary to build a road up the Harrison River valley to the upper reaches of the Fraser. In 1857 Captain Palliser, carrying out surveys for a proposed road through the Rockies, had found the Kicking Horse Pass, and in 1865 Walter Moberly, the assistant surveyor general of British Columbia, had proposed a route through the Eagle Pass and following the 'big bend' of the Columbia River to the Howse Pass and the head of the North Saskatchewan River. The official surveys conducted by Fleming concentrated on the established Yellowhead Pass route, with Burrard Inlet as the ultimate destination. Marcus Smith, principal assistant engineer in British Columbia, started from Bute Inlet, favored by many westerners as offering a bridging point to Vancouver Island and a terminus at Victoria. He proposed a route through the Homathko canyon, along the Chilko River to its junction with the Fraser, then north to the Pine River Pass, between the 55th and 56th parallels. In 1878 the government finally settled on the Yellowhead Pass route to a terminus on Burrard Inlet. Fleming, his work completed, returned to England and ultimate retirement.

This was not the end of the story as far as the mountain route was concerned, but 1878 marked the completion of the survey as a whole, and the mountain section had been by no means the most difficult. North of Lake Superior, the survey parties had to contend with forest, innumerable rivers and streams, and treacherous muskeg swamps in attempting to find a suitable location for the railway. The Grand Trunk had ruled itself out of the competition to build the railway precisely because of the government's insistence on locating it north of the Great Lakes, rather than across US territory south of Lake Superior. The company argued that such an undertaking was impossible, but the original choice of three routes, one to the north and two to the south of Lake Nipigon, was settled in favor of one of the latter, following the shore of Lake Superior to Thunder Bay, then west to a crossing of the Red River at Selkirk, some miles north of Winnipeg.

Once these decisions had been reached it was possible to begin building. The immensity of the survey task is indicated by the fact that it took up to 2,000 men to complete it over a period of six years, working with admirable efficiency. However, building was supposed

to have started within two years, and many westerners were becoming impatient. The obvious starting places were those points where materials could be delivered by water or where immediate commercial dividends might be reaped, but the problem was there were no obvious builders. Charters had been granted in 1872 to both the Interoceanic and the Canada Pacific Railway Companies, but attempts to combine these were ultimately frustrated by the Pacific Scandal of 1873, when it became known that the prime minister, Sir John A. Macdonald, had been involved in questionable financial transactions with one of the organisers of the new company. In the resulting general election Alexander Mackenzie's Liberal party was elected to office. Rather than pursue the Conservative administration's goal of finding a private company to undertake the work, Mackenzie, in his secondary role as Minister of Public Works, began to place contracts for

the construction of the first sections, with Sandford Fleming as Chief Engineer.

The first contracts, awarded in 1874, were for a line from Winnipeg south along the Red River to Pembina, where in 1878 it formed a connection with the St Paul and Pacific Railroad. The river had long been the main means of access to the Red River settlement, and the completion of the railway saw the city grow rapidly. The second series of contracts concerned a line from Fort William, on Lake Superior, west to the Red River. Started in 1875, this line was completed early in 1880 and scheduled services began in February of that year. With the railway connection between Winnipeg and the United States established, it was possible to start on a line westward from Winnipeg, the first contracts being placed in 1879. Finally, a start was made on the west coast in the same year, with the first contracts awarded to Andrew Onderdonk: by 1882 Onderdonk had been given

involving the St Paul and Pacific's metamorphosis into the St Paul, Minneapolis and Manitoba that had netted huge profits for the syndicate. In February 1881 the company received the approval of the House of Commons.

It was clear from the example of the first American transcontinental railroad, the Union Pacific and Central Pacific, that extraordinary qualities were needed in the men who built them. In addition to a large dose of good luck, a combination of financial genius and ruthlessness at headquarters, along with exceptional organisational ability in the field, were essential. In the case of the Canadian Pacific the financial acumen was provided by Stephen and the ruthlessness in large measure by Hill, whose first step was to reject the route west of Winnipeg selected by Fleming. He despatched Major A. B. Rogers to survey a series of passes to the south of the Yellowhead, the intention being to find a more

Below: Lord Mount Stephen, formerly George Stephen, the first president of the Canadian Pacific Railway from the company's formation in February 1881.

responsibility for building a total of 212 miles from Port Moody, near the mouth of Burrard Inlet, up the Fraser and Thompson Rivers to Savona's Ferry, on Kamloops Lake.

All these sections, useful as they were, represented no more than a fraction of the total distance to be covered, and the return to power of Macdonald and the Conservatives in late 1878 brought a resumption of the search for a company to build and operate the Pacific railway in its entirety. This time the search was successful. The Canadian Pacific company was formed, its principal directors being George Stephen and R. B. Angus, former president and general manager of the Bank of Montreal; Donald McIntyre, manager of the Canada Central Railway; Donald A. Smith, a prominent politician and senior Hudson's Bay Company official; and James J. Hill, a Canadian who had started as a steamship operator on the Red River and who had masterminded the financial arrangements

Below: Sir William Cornelius Van Horne, general manager of the Canadian Pacific during its construction and successor as president to Lord Mount Stephen.

direct route west from Winnipeg. Among the inducements offered to Rogers was the promise of $5,000 if he should find a suitable pass; and that it would be named after him: among the passes to be investigated was the one known as Kicking Horse, originally explored by Palliser in 1857. This was found by Rogers to offer a difficult but practicable means of access to the pass through the Selkirks which now bears his name, and beyond to the western section building towards Kamloops.

Hill did not have his way over the eastern part of the route, however. When his desire to take the railway south of Lake Superior was finally thwarted he resigned from the syndicate, returning to the northwestern United States to build his own railroad empire. Before doing so, however, he had made another significant contribution to the Canadian Pacific's ultimate success by engaging William Cornelius Van Horne, general manager of the Chicago, Milwaukee and St

Paul Railroad, to take up a similar position with the new enterprise. Van Horne started his new job on the first day of 1882, and soon made the startling announcement that he intended to build 500 miles of track across the prairies before the end of the first summer. He started by engaging 5,000 men and 1,700 teams of horses; he built accommodation trains for the laborers and organised supply trains which each carried a mile's worth of ties, rails and spikes. The ties were loaded on carts at the railhead and distributed ready along the graded roadbed; horse-drawn trolleys carried the rails forward, paused to allow each pair to be positioned on the spaced ties, and then proceeded while they were plated and spiked. By introducing round-the-clock shifts Van Horne pushed the rails forward at the rate of three miles a day, building over 400 miles clear across Saskatchewan, and adding more than a hundred miles of branches in Manitoba to meet his target. During 1883 the rails were extended as far as Calgary by August and on to the Kicking Horse Pass by the end of the year.

The mountain sections involved almost unbelievable difficulties. Between bridges over unpredictable mountain streams, the roadbed often had to be carved out of solid rock, and simply getting the supplies up to the construction teams often involved creating new roads. From the west 7,000 men under

Onderdonk's control were building toward Eagle Pass, using the old Cariboo Trail as a supply road and spending up to $300,000 a mile on the work. Meanwhile, during 1884, another 10,000 men were at work on the equally arduous section to the north of Lake Superior, where costs were even higher. Granite ridges were blasted away and muskegs swallowed as much filling as could be found, as well as, on more than one occasion, the newly laid rails complete with locomotives. An indication of the difficulty is provided by Van Horne's decision to build no less than three dynamite factories in the area to satisfy the needs of the blasters, along with stone quarries to feed the muskegs where temporary trestles would not serve.

In view of the difficulties, progress was impressive – but the cost was enormous. The original terms of the Canadian Pacific contract had stipulated a government subsidy of $25,000,000 plus land grants on the American pattern of alternate sections along the right of way amounting to 25,000,000 acres, as well as the existing lines constructed under government contracts. In addition, the railway was given a number of concessions. No import duty would be charged on materials, no competing lines could be built between the main line and the US border for a period of 20 years, there were important tax concessions and the company would be able to use its land grants as security for loans totalling another $25,000,000. But these subsidies carried important strings: the cash and land were only to be handed over in instalments, the value of the land itself was dependent on the railway's completion, and tax concessions were of little use to a concern heading rapidly for insolvency.

Until 1884 Stephen had managed to keep the company solvent by a variety of stratagems, but by the beginning of 1884 more drastic measures were needed. It was impossible to sell any more stock in a railway that many were coming to think would never be finished, and more than half the government subsidy remained to be earned. It was suggested that the government should lend the company $22,500,000 on the security of the unsold land, the remaining land grants and the railway itself. This was approved, and construction was able to continue but, by the end of the year, with the money running out again, there were still gaps both in British Columbia and in the eastern section between Callander and Port Arthur. Then, when it was becoming politically impossible for the government to provide further support, and it was beginning to seem that the company would collapse almost within sight of its goal, its luck turned.

There had long been hostility between the métis, descendants of the original French settlers in the Red River region, and the new Canadians, and in March·1885 the hostility turned to open rebellion. This was a severe test for the Dominion government – which needed to show that it could maintain order – and a golden opportunity for the railway to show how it could help. By the end of the month a force of 3,000 soldiers was ready to move west, and by an astonishing feat of organisation Van Horne was able to have the first detachments at Winnipeg within five days. Gaps between the rails were crossed by horse-drawn sleighs, hot meals were provided at the transfer points, and the move was carried out with hardly a break. The rebellion was not finally ended until July, but the Canadian Pacific had done all it could, and rather more than could have been expected. The government was able to gain support for further assistance to the railway, and Van Horne declared that the railway should erect a monument to Louis Riel, the unfortunate leader of the rebellion.

With renewed resources the work was pressed to a rapid conclusion. On November 7 Donald Smith drove home an iron·spike at a spot named Craigellachie in the Eagle Pass to mark the completion of the main line, five days after the last gap on the eastern section had been filled, and on the following day the train carrying Smith and Van Horne arrived

Below: Troops on board a Canadian Pacific train en route to suppress the Riel rebellion and clinch government backing for the CP's completion in April 1885.

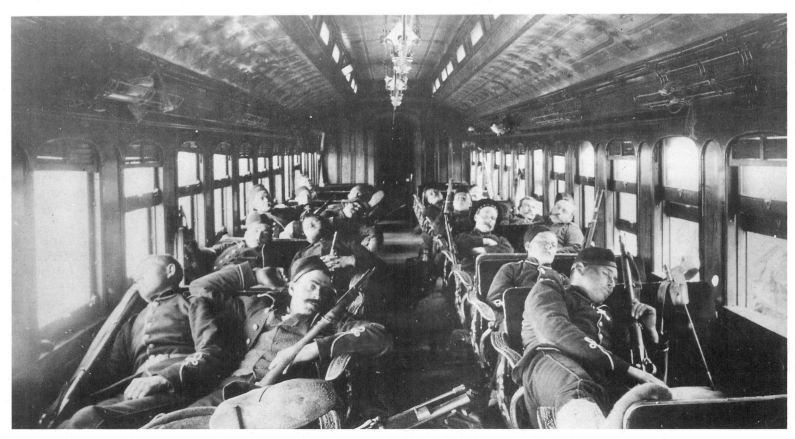

Inset: Cover of a commemorative folder produced by the Bank Note Company of Canada to mark the inauguration of regular services on the transcontinental in June 1886.

Below: Donald A. Smith, later Lord Strathcona, drives home the ceremonial last spike at Craigellachie, British Columbia, on November 7, 1885.

at Port Moody. Regular traffic through the mountains began the following spring, and on June 28, 1886, the Pacific Express, the first regular train from Montreal to Port Moody, left Dalhousie Square Station.

The original terminus of the Pacific railway had been established as Callander, at the eastern end of Lake Nipissing, but it was hardly to be expected that a railway company would be content to build a line more than 2,000 miles from the Pacific coast to the middle of nowhere. At an early stage the Canadian Pacific had taken control of the Canada Central, extending its Ottawa–Pembroke main line 120 miles to Callander. In 1882 the western part of the Quebec, Montreal, Ottawa and Occidental Railway, built by the provincial government of Quebec, was added, providing a line between Ottawa and Montreal and through connection to Quebec City. By the beginning of 1884 a network of lines had been built up in Ontario and

Above: A turn-of-the-century scene at Hamilton, Ontario, with a passenger train halted at the Toronto, Buffalo and Lake Huron Railway station.

Left: Westbound train No 11 at Calgary Alberta – then the Northwest Territories – in 1884, shortly after the inauguration of services to the city.

Below: D9c class 4–6–0 locomotive No 579 at the head of the Canadian Pacific's Trans-Canada Limited near Lake Louise, Alberta, in the early 1920s.

Facing page, top: May 1905: employees of the Toronto, Hamilton and Buffalo Railway, operated jointly by CP and the New York Central until the latter's bankruptcy.

Facing page, inset: Front and back covers of a pocket time card issued by the Western Division of Canadian Pacific and showing the services in effect from July 3, 1886.

eastern Quebec through the acquisition of the Ontario and Quebec, the Toronto, Grey and Bruce, the London Junction and the Credit Valley Railways. Following a conflict with the Grand Trunk over its expanding activities in the area, the Canadian Pacific added the North Shore Railway, which connected the Quebec, Montreal, Ottawa and Occidental with Quebec City.

During the next 15 years the company steadily increased its network in Ontario and Quebec. One of the most important extensions was the direct line to the Atlantic coast, achieved by a combination of the acquisition of existing lines and the construction of new ones. Thus a link between the South-Eastern Railway at Farnham and the south end of the new St Lawrence bridge (opened in 1887) gave direct access to eastern Quebec. Further

Above: Part of the miles of snow sheds needed on the Canadian Pacific's original Rocky Mountain route before tunnels were built to bypass the stretches at risk from avalanches.

Facing page: Construction of the Lethbridge Viaduct on the Canadian Pacific's new route west through the Crow's Nest Pass. The viaduct, the highest in Canada, was completed in 1909.

additions in the form of the International Railway between Lennoxville and Megantic, and the Waterloo and Magog between the former town and Sherbrooke, brought Canadian Pacific traffic to the border of Maine, and to Newport, Vermont, where there were connecting services with Boston. From Megantic a new line was built to Mattawamkeag, in Maine, and the incorporation of the New Brunswick system gave direct access over Maine Central tracks to Saint John and, by a traffic exchange agreement with the Intercolonial, to Halifax, both over routes considerably shorter than those operated by the older company.

In southeastern Ontario, too, the position was improved. Rationalisation of access to Ottawa, Montreal and Toronto by the creation of new stretches of connecting lines was followed by extensions to London and Windsor. A new line to Sault Ste Marie was accompanied by the takeover of the Minnesota, St Paul and Pacific and the Duluth, South Shore and Atlantic systems in the northwestern United States and new traffic agreements with the Midwestern systems.

Similarly, the network in the prairies was extended rapidly, short local railways combining with hundreds of miles of new branches. In addition, a new international connection was achieved at Portal, where new branches of the Canadian Pacific and the Minnesota, St Paul and Sault Ste Marie met. On the Pacific coast, too, there were extensions, including the nine miles from Port Moody to the mouth of Burrard Inlet, where the city of Vancouver would grow up as a result, and a branch south from Mission to an international connection with the Northern Pacific. The Esquimalt and Nanaimo Railway, on the island of Vancouver, had been completed in 1886. Following its purchase by

Canadian Pacific in 1905, the existing line between Victoria and Wellington was extended to Courtenay, and branches added to Port Alberini and Lake Cowichan. The original purpose of this line had been to connect the mainland section of the Canadian Pacific with the proposed terminal at Esquimalt, when it was thought that the transcontinental would be built to Bute Inlet with a bridge to the island, but connections have been provided by train ferries from Vancouver instead. A more ambitious shipping service had been inaugurated in 1891, when regular sailings were started from Halifax to Shanghai, Hong Kong, and Yokohama, scheduled to take $30\frac{1}{2}$ days in winter and two days less in summer and laying the foundations of the company's global transport network.

In parallel with this process of expansion, there was continuing improvement to the original main line, including double-tracking of the important grain route between Winnipeg and Fort William in 1905–08. It was in the mountains, however, that the most dramatic improvements were effected. Extensive snowsheds were erected to protect the line from avalanches, and facilities were improved, but there was also new construction and some more fundamental revisions which, because of the nature of the terrain, involved some spectacular feats of engineering.

One of these was a result of the railway's exploitation of the Crow's Nest, the most southerly Canadian pass through the Rockies, on the border between Alberta and British Columbia and less than 50 miles north of the international boundary. This was an area of vital interest, particularly because of the high proportion of American settlers in the area and the attractions such a mineral-rich district held for Jim Hill's growing network south of the border. The Canadian Pacific began by leasing the Alberta Railway and Coal Company's line from Dunsmore, a few miles west of Medicine Hat, to Lethbridge, buying it outright four years later. Then, with the help of a government subsidy, the line was extended through the pass, where further short lines were acquired and linked to form a series of branches into the Kootenay and Elk valleys. The line through the Crow's Nest was opened in 1899, but it was another 10 years before the most impressive structure on the line was completed, in the shape of the 5,327ft-long Lethbridge viaduct carrying the line 314ft above the Belly River, and the highest railway bridge in Canada.

Meanwhile, operating conditions on the original main line through the Kicking Horse and Rogers Passes were proving something of a nightmare. Between Field and Hector, on an eight-mile stretch known as the 'Big Hill', stretches of grades between 3.5 and 4.4 percent meant that westbound trains climbing up to the pass had to be divided into sections for the ascent. Freight trains working down the hill were restricted to six miles an hour, while the brakemen ran alongside to watch for slipping or overheating wheels. The solution came in the form of the famous spiral tunnels, one 3,255ft long, with a turn of 291 degrees under Cathedral Mountain, and the other – the second for westbound trains – turning through 217 degrees in a distance of 2,992ft under Mount Ogden. In the process the line drops by a total of 105ft, and

the increase in distance allowed the ruling grade to be reduced to 2.2 percent. The tunnels were completed in August 1909 and resulted in considerably easier conditions, but they still demanded additional helper engines for the climb over the pass.

Further to the west, the Rogers Pass presented difficulties of a different kind. The original route was restricted to 2.2 percent grades from the start, but in the process followed a very twisting course, and during the winter operations were frequently interrupted by avalanches. The solution here was the excavation of the double-track Connaught Tunnel, five miles long under the summit of Mount Macdonald. Its effects included a reduction in the line's maximum height from 4,340ft to 3,787ft, the elimination of 2,500 degrees of difficult curves along with four miles of snowsheds, and a reduction in distance of $4\frac{1}{4}$ miles. Its completion in 1916 was the result of three years' work.

A line between Fort Steele, on the Crow's Nest line, and Golden, on the main line between the Kicking Horse and Rogers Passes, saw the British Columbia part of the system substantially complete, and by this stage there had been further acquisitions in the east. Steady growth in traffic led to the construction of the Sudbury–Toronto line, connecting with the branch from the new Georgian Bay terminus for Great Lakes traffic at Port McNicoll. Another line was built from Agincourt, to the east of Toronto, to Glen Tay, where a double-tracked line continued east to Montreal. In the Montreal area, in eastern Quebec and in the maritimes, many local lines were leased. Among them was the Dominion Atlantic Railway in Nova Scotia, which provided a connection from Truro to Halifax via Windsor, and from Windsor to Yarmouth. Further lines were acquired in New Brunswick, all contributing to increased traffic and providing additional international connections.

However, the most relentless expansion in the years before the First World War took place in the prairies, as the bulk of the traffic that justified such expansion in the east originated from there. The company pursued its active policy of land settlement in the early years of the century, and as new strains of wheat allowed the agricultural frontier to be pushed steadily north, new branches and connections were bought or built, reaching south of the original main lines towards the international boundary, and north into Saskatchewan and Alberta. Between Winni-

peg and Calgary the web of lines spread out from the border in the south to Prince Albert and Edmonton in the north, and the double tracking of the main line was extended west to Portage la Prairie and Regina.

The complementary effects of increasing settlement and improving rail connections were reflected in the traffic carried by the railway. Although grain crops were always at the mercy of climatic and other factors, so that yearly totals fluctuated, the general trend showed a steady increase. In 1885, the railway's year of completion, its total mileage was 4,338 by 1892. This had passed 6,000 and reached 7,000 in 1899, while during the same period total freight carried was almost quadrupled from nearly 11 million tons in 1886 to over 42 million in 1899. With considerable fluctuations caused by variable harvests, the growth of traffic continued into the new century before being disrupted by the effects of the First World War; total freight carried reached 20 million tons by 1910 and 30 million in 1920, the peak year being 1917, when over 31 million tons were carried. The contribution made by grain to these totals was 11 million bushels in 1886, 20 million in 1890, 42 million in 1899, 112 million in 1910 and 172 million in 1920. The peak year was 1916, with nearly 277 million bushels. All this was accompanied by a steady increase in efficiency, the use of heavier rails and improved equipment allowing average train loads to pass the 200-ton mark toward the end of the century, 400 tons in 1912, and 577 tons by 1920.

The prosperity engendered by this record of growth was sustained until the onset of worldwide depression at the end of the 1920s,

Above: A new line south from Moose Jaw into southern Saskatchewan, one of the many grain feeders built by Canadian Pacific after completion of the main line.

Facing page, top: Construction work around the entrance to the Canadian Pacific's Connaught Tunnel, brought into use in December 1916 to eliminate the final climb up to Rogers Pass.

Facing page, below: The five-mile long, double tracked Connaught Tunnel reduced the climb to Rogers Pass by 552 ft (168 m) and eliminated six full circles of turns and four miles of track

Top right: Dining car on the train used by King George VI and Queen Elizabeth for the royal tour of Canada during the spring and early summer of 1919.

Above right: Observation car of the train used by the royal party for their tour, which came as brief diversion between the years of depression and the Second World War.

Top left: Among the attractions for travellers on Canadian Pacific were the hotels such as the Banff Springs Hotel in Alberta, seen here in the late 1920s.

Above left: Golf is the attraction offered in this list of Canadian Pacific hotels, reverse of the Chateau Lake Louise lunch menu for June 7, 1919.

though without the spectacular expansion of earlier years. But the worldwide slump in business activity and demand for commodities affected the Canadian Pacific as severely as it did other railways, so that in 1932 the company was forced to suspend dividends. Indeed, the situation was so serious that a Royal Commission was established in 1931 to examine the whole structure of Canada's railways, with particular reference to the competition between the Canadian Pacific and the national system established ten years earlier. There were few tangible results of the Commission's deliberations and the subsequent legislation, beyond the formation of joint committees and the pooling of passenger traffic between Montreal and Toronto, but the enforced cooperation helped both systems to survive until economic conditions began to improve in the late 1930s.

The Second World War brought new problems, though this time the main difficulty was meeting the unprecedented demands of wartime production and troop movements, particularly to the Atlantic ports of Saint John and Halifax. Record totals were reached in both freight and passenger movements, despite the loss of many experienced employees to the armed forces and the use of

Above: Canadian Pacific locomotive No 209, and Atlantic type 4–4–2.

Above: One of the 2800 Class 4–6–4 Hudson locomotives introduced in 1928 and used to haul the transcontinental passenger expresses at an average 33 mph.

regular steam operations had been finished for six months.

Many steam locomotives had been built in Canadian Pacific's own shops, but for diesel traction the company turned to the established manufacturers, notably MLW in Montreal and General Motors of Canada's Diesel Division at London, Ontario. By the time the conversion was complete, the railway had well over a thousand locomotives at work in the yard and on the line. At the beginning of 1982, when GMD had completed delivery of

Previous page: Canadian Pacific locomotive No 2327, a 4–6–2 Pacific type, hauls the Trans-Canada Limited out of Windsor Station, Montreal, at the start of its journey to the Pacific in 1926.

Above: Inside the caboose of a Toronto, Hamilton and Buffalo freight train, possibly in the 1940s: the conductor consults his train orders.

engineering facilities for the fabrication of military hardware. Dividend payments were resumed in 1944, but the boom generated by the war had the effect of masking some more fundamental challenges to the position of railways in the economy.

These new challengers were the airplane, the bus and, overwhelmingly, the private automobile for passenger transport and the combination of truck and pipeline for freight. In 1938, when just over 50 billion ton miles of freight were moved in Canada, the railways took just over half, roads took just under three percent, and the remainder was waterborne. By the last year of the war, railways had increased their share of the 88 billion ton miles to nearly 72 percent, while water transport accounted for only a quarter. During the next ten years, however, when the total increased again to 127 billion tons, pipelines had taken a ten percent share, marginally less than that carried by road, reducing the railways' share to 52 percent. Subsequently, while water transport has recovered slightly to account for around a third, rail traffic has declined toward a similar figure.

The railways' response to such trends could only be increased efficiency and, as far as the Canadian Pacific was concerned, the most obvious answer was a rapid switch from steam to diesel motive power. The railway had acquired its first diesel locomotive as early as 1937, but it was another 12 years before this yard switcher was followed by the first road diesel. The complete takeover by diesels took little more than another decade: the last steam-hauled train to run on Canadian Pacific tracks was a special from Montreal to St Lin on November 6, 1960, and by then

Right: Double-headed Canadian Pacific passenger train with one of the massive 2–10–4 Selkirk type locomotives built for service west of Calgary leading the way.

75 3,000hp SD40-2s – costing $75 million, and the biggest order in the company's history – the total of road freight locomotives stood at 566. Of these, 80 were MLW engines delivered in 1968–71, comprising 35 3,000hp DRF-30s, 44 3,300hp DRF-36s and a single 4,000hp DRF-36d. The remainder were General Motors designs, comprising 65 SD40s delivered in 1966–67 and 421 SD40-2s built in the ten years since 1972, all of 3,000hp. The roster also included 467 road switchers of various MLW and GMD models and 192 yard switchers, as

well as a total of 34 GMD FP7A, F7B and F9B locomotives dating from the early 1950s, some of which were among the first candidates for a ten-year, $200 million rebuilding programme initiated in 1980.

The conversion to diesel power formed the prelude to major reorganisations of the railway's corporate structure. In 1961 the United States subsidiaries – the Minneapolis, St Paul and Sault Ste Marie, the Duluth, South Shore and Atlantic and the Wisconsin Central, the last of which had been leased by the

appropriate divisions. An addition to the CP Rail network came in 1977 with the Toronto, Hamilton and Buffalo Railway. It had previously been operated jointly by CP Rail and the New York Central, following the latter's merger with the Pennsylvania Railroad in 1968, the bankruptcy of the resulting Penn-Central system and the formation of Conrail to pick up the pieces in 1976; CP Rail acquired full ownership in April 1977.

Meanwhile, the need for improved efficiency had inspired a series of develop-

A variety of liveries on late-1960s CP freight equipment: two 2,400hp DRS-24c locomotives, a 50ft single-door box car (green) and a 50ft, 70-ton refrigerated car.

Bottom: A mixed freight train emerges from the downhill end of one of the spiral tunnels between Hector and Field on the Kicking Horse Pass section of the route.

Minneapolis line in 1909 – were amalgamated to form the new Soo Line Railroad Company. This rationalisation created a substantial system in the United States west of the Great Lakes with a direct line to Chicago, and was followed in 1971 by more fundamental changes. In that year the continuing diversification of the original company was recognised by the change of name to CP Rail and its new status as one of several components of Canadian Pacific Limited, whose other activities were similarly organised into

Canadian Pacific F2a Class 4-4-4 locomotive No 3000, built by the Montreal Locomotive Works and delivered to the railway in July 1936.

ments. In parallel with the switch to diesel power Canadian Pacific began a comprehensive modernisation and automation of its freight yards. The first modern hump yard in Canada, with fully mechanised retarders for car sorting, was opened at St Luc, Montreal, in 1950. Subsequently this yard, along with those at Agincourt, Toronto and Alyth, Calgary, became fully computer controlled as far as the switching and speed of individual cars is concerned. The YARD (yard activity reporting and decision) system installed at Vancouver in 1975–78, and extended to Thunder Bay in 1980, takes the process a stage further with computerised management of all cars being extended to include the planning of train consists. New controls being installed at Calgary and Toronto will also be integrated with the YARD system, and movement of all cars on CP Rail tracks is monitored from the company's Montreal headquarters.

Bottom: Towards the end of the steam era, a Toronto, Hamilton and Buffalo locomotive No 102 at work switching freight cars onto a railway barge or ferry.

Computerisation, like other modern freight handling techniques, is not unique to CP Rail, but the company has pursued some of these with commendable vigor. Automation has been extended not only to such areas as the cleaning of refrigerator cars, among the wide variety of specialised freight cars op-

erated, but also to train operations. An outstanding example of this is provided by the unit trains used for the transport of bulk cargoes, notably coal. CP Rail's first unit train was used to carry sulphur in 1967, and in 1970 the concept was applied to the ferrying of coal over the 700 miles between Spar-

wood, in the Crow's Nest Pass area, to the Roberts Bank port, south of Vancouver, for export to Japan. The 10 trains used on this route each consist of 11 3,000hp locomotives coupled in blocks with 88 or 105 gondola cars; each carries 115.7 metric tons of coal, enabling the transportation of a staggering eight

Above: Canadian Pacific's Canadian transcontinental, introduced in 1955, featured stainless steel cars and provided the longest dome car journey in the world – 3,045 miles (4,900 km).

Three GMD SD40-2 3,000hp locomotives of the DRF-30 Class head a unit train of empty hopper cars along a river valley on a sunlit winter's day.

Above: Computer-controlled car retarders on the hump at Alyth: precise pressure must be applied, taking into account the car's weight, speed and route to the classification track.

Right: General Motors 1,000 hp Model NW2 diesel locomotive, one of four of this type supplied to the Toronto, Hamilton and Buffalo Railway in 1947.

million tons each year. Another three million tons are moved annually by three 104-car trains from the Fording mine to Roberts Bank, and in 1978 105-car trains began operation on the 2,600-mile round trip between Corbin, British Columbia, and Thunder Bay, as part of a contract with Ontario Hydro involving 22.5 million tons over 15 years.

Other modern techniques of freight movement involve the ubiquitous container. CP Rail has major container ports at Saint John and Montreal, the former capable of handling 100,000 containers a year, as well as a network of inland container yards where 'piggyback' transfers, involving the carrying of highway trailers on flat cars for rapid transshipment, are available. The emphasis on freight transport was a necessary response to the collapse in demand for passenger transport in the years after the Second World War, which culminated in both CP Rail and Canadian National handing over their passenger services to the government's new VIA Rail concern in 1979. The immense tonnage shifted each year – a total of nearly 94 billion tons in 1981, which fell to just under 85 billion tons in 1982 as a result of economic recession – has demanded an intensive program of track maintenance and modernisation, as well as the purchase of equipment, but the most ambitious of all track improvement projects has been delayed because of difficulties with one of the railway's fundamental cargoes, and one bound up with the whole history of the line.

The government subsidies which enabled the Crow's Nest Pass line to be built at the end of the last century were conditional on reduced rates for the eastbound transport of grain. Rates were subject to alteration until

1925, when a new federal law fixed the rate for the eastbound carriage of grain at half a cent per ton mile, extended to cover all railways and subsequently applied to western ports as well as to Churchill on Hudson Bay. The fact that the rates remained unchanged for more than fifty years, resulted in grain becoming increasingly uneconomic, so that in 1980, for example, grain amounted to 21 percent of total traffic, and was responsible for a $115 million operating loss. The company calculates that the rate paid for shipment covered only one fifth of the actual operating cost.

At the same time, the old main line through the Rogers Pass had become more and more of a bottleneck affecting all operations west of Calgary. As part of a major exercise aimed at easing traffic congestion in the area, substantial progress had been made in reducing heavy grades and double-tracking stretches of the line between Calgary and Vancouver, but the most important part of all involves the planned supplementing of the old Connaught Tunnel with a new nine-mile tunnel under Mount Macdonald. In conjunction with 21 miles of new roadbed, with a total of ten miles in tunnels and using 11 miles of new bridges, the scheme will allow ruling grades to be reduced to one percent, so that while empty trains heading east will continue to use the more heavily graded existing route, loaded trains will be able to negotiate the westbound route without the extensive use of helper locomotives which the current route demands.

The estimates of the project's cost, some $600 million, combined with the depressed demand during the recession of the early 1980s, made such vast expenditure out of the question while so much freight had to be carried at loss-making rates. In 1983, however, agreement was finally reached on a scheme to phase out the old rates, and embodied in the Western Grain Transportation Act, proclaimed in November of that year. Export grain rates will double by 1986, rising further to cover costs completely by the early 1990s, and in the meantime government subsidies will be provided to make up the losses, estimated at a combined total for CP Rail and Canadian National of $659 million in 1984 alone.

As well as enabling the Rogers Pass project to go ahead, the new agreement should justify investment in improved grain-handling equipment, so that unit trains of hopper cars may be the rule in the future.

Massive freight trains now
run through the Kicking
Horse Pass, part of Canadian
Pacific's original trans-
continental main line
through the Rocky
Mountains.

Above: Cathedral Mountain towers over a   Multiple diesel unit emerging from the Connaught Tunnel.

YUKON TERRITORY

DISTRICT OF MACKENZIE

Churchi

BRITISH COLUMBIA

ALBERTA

SASKATCHEWAN

Lynn Lake

Thompson

MANIT

Mc. Murray

Flin Flon

Hines Creek

Dawson Creek

Meadowlake

Prince Albert

Hudson Bay

Terrace

Smithers

Edmonton

Wetaskiwin

Yorkton

Dauphin

Prince Rupert

Endako

Prince George

Edson

Lacombe

Saskatoon

Portage La Prarie

Jasper

Red Deer

Lake Louise

Banff

Calgary

Moose Jaw

Regina

Macgreg

Brandon

Swift Current

Medicine Hat

Estevan

Ft. Macleod

Lethbridge

Kelowna

Vancouver

Penticton

Yahk

Bismark

Victoria

KEY

CANADIAN NATIONAL

CANADIAN PACIFIC

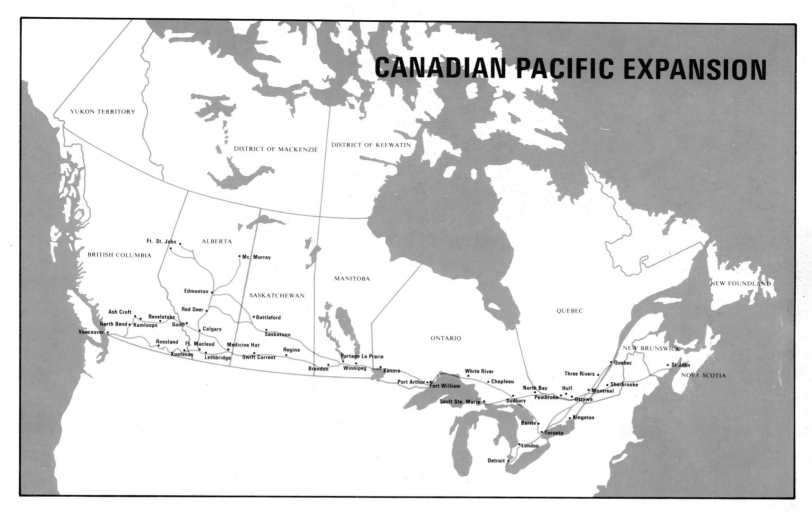

CANADIAN PACIFIC EXPANSION

YUKON TERRITORY

DISTRICT OF MACKENZIE

DISTRICT OF KEEWATIN

NEW FOUNDLAND

BRITISH COLUMBIA

ALBERTA

Ft. St. John

Mc. Murray

MANITOBA

QUEBEC

Edmonton

SASKATCHEWAN

Ash Croft

Revelstoke

Red Deer

North Bend

Kamloops

Banff

Battleford

Vancouver

Calgary

Saskatoon

ONTARIO

NEW BRUNSWICK

Rossland

Ft. Macleod

Medicine Hat

Kootenay

Lethbridge

Swift Current

Regina

NOVA SCOTIA

Brandon

Winnipeg

Kenora

Portage La Prarie

Quebec

St John

White River

Three Rivers

Sherbrooke

Port Arthur

Fort William

Chapleau

North Bay

Hull

Montreal

Sault Ste. Marie

Sudbury

Pembroke

Ottawa

Barrie

Kingston

Toronto

London

Detroit

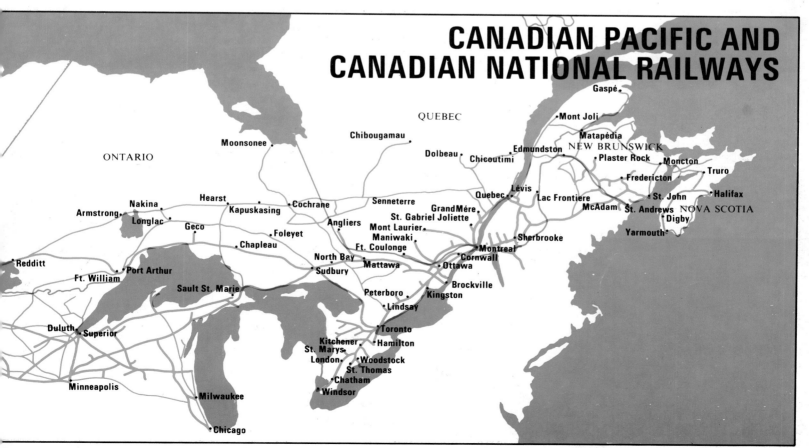

CANADIAN PACIFIC AND
CANADIAN NATIONAL RAILWAYS

Gaspé

Mont Joli

QUEBEC

Matapédia

Chibougamau

Moonsonee

Edmundston

NEW BRUNSWICK

Dolbeau

Plaster Rock

Moncton

ONTARIO

Chicoutimi

Truro

Fredericton

Lévis

Hearst

Senneterre

Quebec

Lac Frontiere

St. John

Halifax

Nakina

Cochrane

GrandMére

McAdam

St. Andrews

NOVA SCOTIA

Armstrong

Kapuskasing

St. Gabriel Joliette

Digby

Longlac

Geco

Angliers

Mont Laurier

Sherbrooke

Yarmouth

Foleyet

Maniwaki

Chapleau

Ft. Coulonge

Montreal

Redditt

North Bay

Mattawa

Cornwall

Ft. William

Port Arthur

Sudbury

Ottawa

Sault St. Marie

Brockville

Peterboro

Kingston

Lindsay

Duluth

Superior

Toronto

Kitchener

Hamilton

St. Marys

Minneapolis

London

Woodstock

St. Thomas

Milwaukee

Chatham

Windsor

Chicago

In the first 15 years of the 20th century, the total mileage of Canadian railways all but doubled, rising from 17,657 in 1900 to 34,882 in 1915. This was a reflection of a general increase in prosperity, as farm prices rose and the drain of emigration was replaced by a net increase in population amounting to 35 percent in the first decade of the century. It also reflected the policies of the new Liberal administration led by Sir Wilfred Laurier, elected in 1896 and not defeated until 1911; and, not least, the activities of Donald Mann and William Mackenzie, who had met while carrying out contracts for the Canadian Pacific in the Kicking Horse Pass, and who in January 1896 embarked on the construction of the Lake Manitoba Railway.

With the help of guarantees from a provincial legislature eager to escape the monopoly of the Canadian Pacific, the first line was opened between Gladstone and Winnipegosis in January 1897. Although this was supposed to be the first stage of a line to the Hudson Bay port on which the prairie settlers were so keen, the partners' next venture was the Manitoba and South Eastern Railway whose charter, like that of their original venture, carried substantial land grants and attracted further provincial guarantees. The onset of winter in 1898 found 45 miles of the new line completed, between Boniface and Marchand, and a pattern of operations that was to characterize the Mackenzie and Mann railways. Construction costs were kept to a minimum, rolling stock was obtained second-hand, and traffic was improvised. Between Gladstone and Winnipegosis the train would stop anywhere; between St Boniface and Marchand, where there was hardly anyone to stop for, firewood was cut and stockpiled in the summer to be carried to Winnipeg in the winter. In their plans for expansion they demonstrated a skill in the acquisition and manipulation of charters, and their associated grants and guarantees, that would form the basis for a national network.

In the first place, federal authority was obtained to change the direction of the line to Hudson Bay, which would now be built to Prince Albert in the rather more promising farming country to the west. With this new direction, and new, more lucrative land grants, the line gained a new name, becoming the Canadian Northern Railway in January 1899. In order to reach Thunder Bay, meanwhile, they bought three more companies, one in Minnesota and two in Ontario, which between them authorized a route across US territory to the south of Lake of the Woods and back across the border to Port Arthur, a link which was completed by the end of 1902. By this time further additions had come in the form of Northern Pacific branches in southern Manitoba, including the useful connection from Winnipeg to Emerson, on the US border, and with the construction of some linking lines the new railway rapidly assumed substantial proportions. Moreover, with their outlet to the Great Lakes, Mann and Mackenzie were in a position to undercut

the Canadian Pacific's grain rates, immediately cementing their popularity in the province.

Their ambitions were much more than provincial, however. New branches in Manitoba followed the developing pattern of settlement, but they also followed it across the border into Saskatchewan and Alberta, a northern branch from Swan River heading for Prince Albert, while a new main line headed west from Dauphin all the way to Edmonton, reached in December 1905. All this was helped by provincial and federal aid in the form of fresh guarantees and land grants. At the same time, a small network of over 400 miles had been bought and built in Nova Scotia, and in 1904 the Great Northern Railway of Canada brought another 244 miles in Quebec, including a line from Quebec to Montreal and Hawkesbury, into the group.

The result was that by 1907 the Canadian Northern had grown to a total of 2,640 miles in little more than 10 years. Already a line from Toronto to Sudbury was under way, and the outlines of a transcontinental system were becoming clear, but the heavy inflation

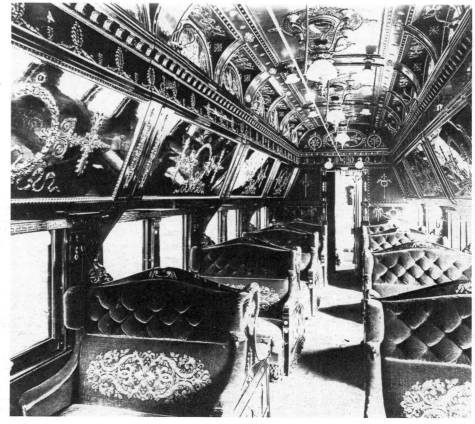

Left: A Canadian Northern freight train passes a row of grain elevators in a typical scene during the railway's brief but spectacular period of expansion in the prairies.

of the period was taking its toll. The brief financial panic of 1907 had slowed the sale of bonds, on which the railway was heavily dependent, and the Canadian Northern, which had begun as an upstart challenger to the prairie monopoly of the Canadian Pacific, was now itself threatened by competition.

Mackenzie and Mann had seized the moment in exploiting the rapid growth in settlement and grain production on the prairies that started at the turn of the century, but just as Manitoba resented the Canadian Pacific monopoly, so there was pressure from the east for a second transcontinental rail-

Below: Canadian National's Continental Limited at Cisco, British Columbia, where CN and Canadian Pacific tracks cross to opposite banks of the Fraser River.

way that would both encourage settlement of northern Quebec and Ontario, and carry the western grain to eastern ports. Sir Wilfred Laurier's government responded by announcing a federal subsidy for a projected line 400 miles long from Roberval, on the Saguenay River, to Nottawa, on James Bay, which would form the first stage of a Trans-Canada Railway. The overall scheme for this railway was somewhat unrealistic, however, its planned route beyond James Bay was too far north to do anybody much good. The Grand Trunk Railway, with a new President in Charles Rivers Wilson, and a new General Manager in Charles Hays, aware that the prosperity of its eastern network was increasingly dependent on western traffic, wanted its own line to the west. This was planned to start from Callander, on Lake Nipissing, and head north then west through the fertile clay belt of northern Ontario and on to Winnipeg, before following Sandford Fleming's old route via Edmonton and the Yellowhead Pass to a new terminal at Port Simpson. A more sensible proposal to embark on a joint venture with Canadian Northern, each railway sticking to its established territory

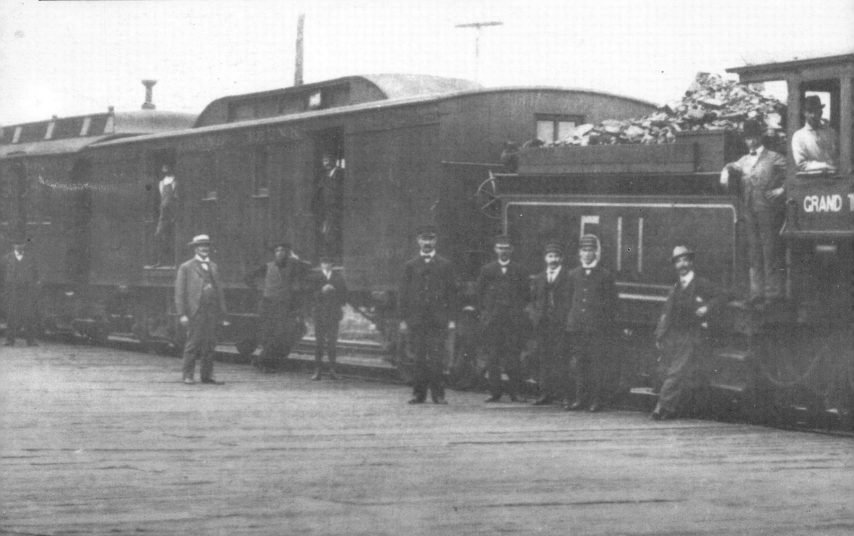

while contributing to a shared line from Port Arthur to North Bay, foundered on the Trunk's determination to take over the Canadian Northern. By March 1903, when the Grand Trunk Pacific Railway was formed, Quebec was ready to abandon the Trans-Canada in favor of the new line if it extended to Quebec, while New Brunswick joined in with a further demand for another extension to Moncton.

By this time the project was entirely out of control, the initial Grand Trunk Pacific plan being risky enough without the extra 900 miles to Moncton. The solution devised by Laurier divided the line in two. The Grand Trunk Pacific would go ahead with the western section of the line from Winnipeg to Port Simpson, while the Grand Trunk itself would build the 1800 miles from Moncton to Winnipeg, at government expense, as the National Transcontinental, and would then operate it under lease from the government. Rivers Wilson was less than enthusiastic about this plan, which Hays had accepted without proper authority, but felt compelled to support it and succeeded in convincing a majority of the Grand Trunk's board in

London. Political opposition was also plentiful, but popular support was reflected in the Liberals' resounding victory in the 1904 general election.

As a result, the surveys for the new railway began in 1905, and given the rigorous specifications for the new line, which was to have maximum grades of 0.4 percent eastbound and 0.6 percent westbound, and a maximum curvature of four degrees, the final location was still not settled when the first construction contracts were awarded a year later. This was reflected in the piecemeal completion of the eastern division. The section between Moncton and Edmunston was opened for operation by the Intercolonial from late 1911, but a through service to the St Lawrence opposite Quebec was not started until 1915. The Quebec Bridge was a saga in itself: plans for it pre-dated the National Transcontinental, and work was started in 1900 by the Phoenix Bridge Company of

Facing page, top: Main line of the Grand Trunk Pacific Railway under construction at Tête Jaune, British Columbia, west of the Yellowhead Pass in 1912.

Below: Locomotive No 511 at the head of a passenger train on the Grand Trunk shortly after the turn of the century, when the railway was at its peak.

Pennsylvania. Following the collapse of the southern span in 1907, when 75 workmen were killed, the federal government took over, and in 1911 the St Lawrence Bridge Company started work to a new design. By September 1916 only the central span remained to be installed, but in a second disaster a casting gave way during the hoisting operation and the span fell into the river, carrying another 10 men to their deaths. A year later a replacement was safely hoisted into place.

West of Quebec the work had proceeded more quickly, the line to the provincial border being completed in 1912, by which time the Ontario section was completed as far as Hearst. The Grand Trunk Pacific had completed a line from Superior Junction, near Sioux Lookout, to Fort William in 1908. It had to wait another two years for the completion of the line to Winnipeg, where the Canadian Northern was able to delay its entry to the city for a time, and the section between Superior Junction and Lake Nipigon was opened in 1912. As with the Canadian Pacific, the line across the Canadian Shield north of Lake Superior was proving the most difficult, and it was late in 1913 before the gap was bridged.

West of Winnipeg, meanwhile, the Grand Trunk Pacific had been started in August 1905, and by the end of 1908 a roadbed as straight and level as any on the continent stretched more than 900 miles across the prairies. Delays in the supply of rails meant that it was another two years before the steel had reached the end of the prairie section at Wolf Creek, though regular services to Edmonton had started in 1910 on a schedule four hours shorter than that of the Canadian Northern. Beyond Wolf Creek another epic of railway building was under way. Prince Rupert had replaced Port Simpson as the Pacific terminal, and construction had started from both ends, but the difficulties encountered in carving a comparatively straight and level route through granite mountains, over precipitous ravines and across mountain torrents were such that it was April 1914, five years after construction had started, before the eastern and western rails met.

One of the special problems in the mountains was the presence in the Yellowhead Pass of two sets of construction crews, for by this time the Canadian Northern was also building toward the Pacific. While extending their network in the prairies, Mackenzie and Mann had always been conscious of the ultimate need for ocean outlets, but while they had made a modest start in the east with the lines in Quebec and Nova Scotia, they had planned to build up the western network to a level that would sustain a full-scale transcontinental system. The precipitate start made by their Grand Trunk rivals had forced them to begin before they were ready, but they set about the task methodically. By 1910 provincial guarantees of bonds had been obtained for new branches in Alberta and Saskatchewan, and for a line through the Yellowhead to Vancouver and Vancouver Island, while Ontario made a grant of two million acres of land along a line between Sudbury and Port Arthur. In the same year they sold some $65 million of bonds, and work was started.

From Port Mann, near the mouth of the Fraser, the Canadian Northern Pacific, as the British Columbia subsidiary was named, paralleled the Canadian Pacific as far as Kamloops. In the process it had to find a way through Hell's Gate Canyon between Boston Bar and Kamloops, a major feat involving extensive tunnelling, the excavation of rock ledges to form the roadbed, and a crossing of the Fraser to stay on the opposite bank from the earlier line. At Kamloops, however, while the Canadian Pacific continued east, the new line turned north along the North Thompson, following this river almost all the way to Yellowhead Pass. The Yellowhead section involved more difficulties, compounded by the fact that the Grand Trunk Pacific was building through it at the same time, but in January 1915 the last spike was driven at Basque.

A year earlier, the last spike had been driven on the eastern link between Ottawa and Port Arthur, where construction had begun in 1911, though it was several months before regular services started. By this time the entire enterprise was in deep trouble. For a start, construction costs had been much greater than estimated: in Hell's Gate Canyon they had reached a staggering $350,000 a mile in places. In Ontario, the land grants had turned out to be useless, since land along the route had been claimed already where it was of any value. Even the prairie branches had become uneconomic, as inflation raised construction costs above the value of the traffic. Meanwhile, the Canadian Northern was committed to paying interest on over $300 million-worth of bonds and, in view of the considerable sums still needed, Mackenzie and Mann had no alternative but to seek more government aid.

The government's terms were severe: in return for guarantees on another $45 million of bonds, they demanded a consolidation of all the partners' interests and a mortgage on the whole company. At this point the task became impossible. Having accepted the government's terms, they had hardly started to sell the new bonds when the First World War put an end to the supply of capital from London; in New York the securities could only be sold at substantial discounts. The government was forced to meet interest payments in accordance with the guarantees, and in the face of a steadily worsening situation appointed a Royal Commission to investigate the company in July 1916.

Meanwhile, even without the Quebec Bridge, the National Transcontinental had cost nearly three times the $50 million estimate; the prairie section of the Grand Trunk Pacific had exceeded its estimates by more than 20 percent; total costs of the mountain section, $832\frac{1}{2}$ miles long, were over $100,000 per mile. The Grand Trunk was saddled with massive debts and faced with the prospect of an annual rent, based on three percent of the construction costs, of nearly $5 million for the National Transcontinental. Yet only a few years earlier it seemed to have turned the corner to prosperity, after years of struggle.

The reorganization implemented by Rivers Wilson and Hays had produced dramatic results. The opening of the St Clair Tunnel between Sarnia and Port Huron in 1891 had been followed by the extension of double tracking from Montreal to Toronto by 1903 and to Sarnia by 1905. In 1897 a new bridge was opened over the Niagara River at Niagara Falls, and in the following year a new superstructure was completed on the Victoria Bridge at Montreal, providing a double track crossing. A consolidation of the Grand Trunk's American subsidiaries came next, starting with the acquisition of the Central Vermont Railway and continuing with the formation of the Grand Trunk Western.

The Grand Trunk had a long-standing interest in the Central Vermont and its string of associated and leased companies, and the reorganization of the company in 1898 left the Canadian company in control of a line

Below: Locomotive No 6319 making its last run on the Grand Trunk Western, the US subsidiary formed to give the Grand Trunk its own direct route to Chicago.

Left: 4–8–4 Northern type
locomotive No 6405 built for
high speed passenger work
on the Grank Trunk
Western Railway by
Montreal Locomotive
Works in 1938.

running south through New England to the port of New London, in Connecticut. Similarly, the Grand Trunk Western was a reorganization of the Michigan subsidiaries which as individual operations were a constant drain on Grand Trunk resources, prompting the formation of the new company in January 1900.

The dawn of the new century was marked by the resumption of payments of full dividends, as operating profits mounted, though the constant need for upgrading of track and equipment, coupled with inflation and other expenses, continued to absorb substantial sums. The fatal lure of the transcontinental project was soon to bring dreams of prosperity to an end, however, and its enormous costs, and consequent huge interest payments, at a time when the First World War was pushing up prices, meant that increased traffic only brought increased losses in 1917. The combined effects of over-ambitious construction and the financial havoc resulting from the war were being felt by Grand Trunk and Canadian Northern alike, and in this context it is difficult not to see the tearing up of

Below: Locomotive No 101 of the Central Railway of Vermont, the New England line partly owned by the Grand Trunk from 1898 and later taken over by Canadian National.

Left: Early days on the Central Vermont: the wood-burning locomotive *Deer* poses for the camera outside the railway's engine sheds with its crew.

the newly laid tracks between Edmonton and the Yellowhead Pass as symbolic. Both railways had been built west from Edmonton, and both had used the same pass through the Rockies, so it was inevitable that for miles at a time the two tracks should run within sight of each other. As a result, during 1916 rails from the Canadian Northern line began to be removed for shipment to France, and by the end of the war some 200 miles of track had disappeared, leaving a single line to be shared by the two railways.

The effect of the building of the two new transcontinental systems had been to double Canada's total railway mileage, but the cost had been fantastic, and the Royal Commission's task was to sort out the resulting chaos. A report by an earlier Royal Commission, published in February 1914, had revealed a sorry story of corruption and mismanage-

Above: Central Vermont diesels at St Albans, Vermont, where the old and current watering systems for the locomotives can be seen for comparison.

Facing page, top: The railway station at St Albans, Vermont, at the northern end of the Central Vermont's line from the Canadian border to New London, Connecticut.

Right: Central Vermont locomotive No 700 was built in 1928, the year after the disastrous floods. The railway was repaired and taken over by CN.

Above: Canadian Northern passengers take the air at an unidentified station while the engineman receives his orders from the dispatcher on the platform.

ment during the construction of the National Transcontinental, which had contributed an average $28,000 a mile to the fearsome costs of that enterprise. In June 1914 the government had passed legislation empowering the Minister of Railways to place the Quebec-Moncton section of the National Transcontinental under government control, operating under the name Canadian Government Railways.

Until this point the maritime section of the National Transcontinental had been operated by the Intercolonial, which for years had been seen as a symbol of the evils of public owner-

ship. Overstaffed with the nominees of local members of Parliament, forced to place contracts to the same members' political and financial advantage, it rarely covered its costs, gaining a dismal reputation which persisted even after David Pottinger, General Manager of the railway for 36 years until his retirement in 1913, had succeeded in eliminating many of the abuses and improving its efficiency. During the First World War the Intercolonial would redeem itself by its performance in handling the unprecedented traffic to Halifax, but it would not survive the war as a separate entity.

by the parent Grand Trunk. As a result, the government provided interim subsidies to the two troubled railways while awaiting the Royal Commission's report.

Of the many alternatives considered by the Commissioners, their recommendation was public ownership of the Grand Trunk, Grand Trunk Pacific and National Transcontinental, along with the Canadian Northern, by a Dominion Railway Company which it was hoped would be independent of political interference, though still subject to the authority of the Board of Railway Commissioners. The means of acquiring control would be different for each group, however. The value, if any, of the remaining 60 percent of Canadian Northern stock was to be decided by arbitration; the Grand Trunk was considered to be worthless, apparently because of its foreign ownership and general unpopularity, compounded by a willingness to pay dividends to English stockholders rather than meet its obligations to the Canadian government.

In May 1918 the arbitrators fixed a price of $10 million for the outstanding Canadian Northern stock – the maximum price that had been established by the government the previous October – and in September a new board was appointed. In December the National Transcontinental and Intercolonial, along with the Prince Edward Island Railway and a few short lines in New Brunswick that had earlier been taken over by the Intercolonial, were placed under the new board's control, and at the same time the combined system was given a new name – Canadian National Railways. Its total mileage was 13,610.

Below: Staff of the Canadian National Railways ticket office in Vancouver, in the days when there were daily departures by through trains to eastern Canada.

The government's interest in the new railways it had supported so lavishly was increasing. During 1913 it had accepted 40 percent of the Canadian Northern group's stock as security for further loans; in 1914 money was advanced to the Grand Trunk Pacific against a mortgage on the railway; and in 1915 the government leased the strategic Fort William branch. It had also suggested that in view of the Grand Trunk Pacific's understandable reluctance to take on the operation of the National Transcontinental, government aid might be found, again on the security of a mortgage on the railway, but this was refused

The takeover of the Grand Trunk was not so straightforward. After prolonged but fruitless negotiations between railway and government, the Grand Trunk Pacific was placed in receivership in March 1919, and in November legislation was finally passed to establish a board of arbitration to assess the value of the Grand Trunk's common stock. The board's verdict, announced in September 1920, that the common stock was worthless was accepted by the government, despite opposition from the stockholders that would continue in various courts for years afterwards. The temporary board that had taken over four months earlier remained in control until the following May, when the remaining Grand Trunk directors resigned and an all-Canadian board was formed.

The next step was the integration of the total of 22,000 miles of government-controlled railways including 1,380 miles in the United States. Following the amalgamation of the Canadian Northern, National Transcontinental and Intercolonial the new system had been run as two divisions, east and west of Port Arthur; David Hanna, formerly General Manager of Canadian Northern, was President. In 1918 a massive wage rise was made by the Canadian Railways War Board to railway employees, following a similar award in the United States, and in 1920 the absorption of the Grand Trunk and Grand Trunk Pacific started. The new system was faced with the simultaneous need for a drastic rationalization of services, the replacement of track and rolling stock, and demands for the completion of prairie branches whose construction had been suspended during the

war. As a result, modest increases in earnings were more than offset by soaring expenses, and accompanied by provincial demands for lower rates. Public ownership was already acquiring a bad name and, in the face of political interference, Hanna resigned. His replacement, Sir Henry Thornton, took office on October 12, 1922 as President and Chairman, and at the end of January 1923 the Grand Trunk formally became part of the Canadian National Railways Company.

Thornton's qualifications for the job were prodigious. He had started his career in 1894 as a civil engineer with the Pennsylvania Railroad, and after serving as General Superintendent of the Long Island Railroad had moved to England as General Manager of the Great Eastern Railway. During the First World War he had served as Director of Railway Transport in France while taking on the added responsibility of Chief Engineer with the Great Eastern. He had been outstandingly popular with his staff in England, and in Canada he achieved a similar reputation, as evidenced by the famous bronze plaques erected in his memory by Canadian National employees after his retirement in 1932 and his death early in the following year.

His other memorial is the railway system he guided for ten years, during which duplications were eliminated, new branches built, and the standard of lines and equipment raised. Among the moves toward more efficient utilization of the network were the abandonment of the Canadian Northern line between Napanee and Toronto, the construction of the Long Lac cutoff east of Lake Nipigon, allowing the shorter National Trans-

continental route to the north of the lake to be used by trains to and from southern Ontario on the former Canadian Northern line; and the final elimination of the duplication between Edmonton and Redpass Junction, to the west of the Yellowhead Pass. The boom in wheat prices was reflected in the extension of the prairie branches, and another branch was built to the south of the National Transcontinental line in Quebec to the Noranda mining district.

At the same time, new locomotive designs were placed in production, new passenger services inaugurated, and there were such innovations as a radio network, broadcasting to specially equipped cars on long-distance passenger trains. Overall, services were improved to such an extent that by the end of the decade competition with the Canadian Pacific was so intense that during the great depression of the early 1930s, when another Royal Commission was appointed to look at possible improvements to the railway system, the Canadian Pacific's president advocated the merger of the two companies.

The 1930s generally were a decade of survival and slow recovery, so that during the Second World War the railways were able to repeat their achievements of 20 years earlier, coping well with the enormous quantities of war production and the huge numbers of military personnel passing through the ports. Again, Halifax was the principal port, and again it was the old Intercolonial line, now under the administration of Canadian National, that coped with

Below: Tanks on flat cars en route to a port in 1945 symbolise the massive industrial and transportation effort made in response to the demands of war.

Locomotives get up steam in the Montreal roundhouse ready for assignment to their day's duties. The advent of diesels put an end to such scenes.

87

the bulk of the traffic. The early installation of centralized traffic control between Moncton and Halifax enabled the average speed of freight trains to be increased by 30 percent, while up to 80 trains a day were operated over the 125-mile section.

The postwar history of Canadian National in many ways parallels that of the Canadian Pacific. The fall-off in passenger traffic, and the increased competition for freight, forced the streamlining of operations, with diesel locomotives replacing steam and new types of freight cars introduced. At the same time, there were considerable additions to Canadian National's network. In 1949 Newfoundland joined the Confederation, its dilapidated railway system joining the mainland system and adding to the cost of maintenance. In 1979 a subsidiary, TerraTransport, was formed to take over all rail and other transport services on the island.

The construction and operation of such extensions as the Hudson Bay Railway, the Great Slave Lake Railway, Northern Alberta Railways and the Alberta Resources Railway are described in subsequent chapters, while another area of expansion was the creation of more subsidiaries to handle the growing transport, communications, real estate and other enterprises. In contrast to Canadian Pacific, Canadian National continued to promote passenger transport until the final takeover of passenger services by VIA Rail; at the same time, it pursued increases in

Left: Microwave communications and computer control of train movements were still a world away when this operator was photographed at work in 1942.

Below: Dome cars were the ideal way to view the spectacular scenery on long-distance journeys, and empty seats did not remain vacant for long.

Right: No 6060, a Ulf Class 4–8–2 Mountain type locomotive built for Canadian National by the Montreal Locomotive Works in 1944, in a series dating back to 1923.

Canadian National locomotive No 6218, a U-2-g Class 4-8-4 of 1942, was the engine used for the last steam-hauled trains on the railway during 1971.

U-2-e Class locomotive No 6169, one of the long series of CN 4-8-4s that started with the U-2-a in 1927 and culminated in the U-2-h Class in 1943–44.

Locomotive No 3603 of the Duluth, Winnipeg and Pacific Railway, a 1,800hp diesel of Class MR-18a built by the Montreal Locomotive Works.

freight services by improvements to track, yard facilities and innovatory systems.

By the early 1980s the system was in a healthy position, though the recession had an adverse effect on earnings as industrial production fell. However, the contract for the supply of coal from the Tumbler Ridge area of British Columbia, which will be moved in conjunction with British Columbia Railway, is the largest single freight contract the company has ever received, and will involve some 10 million tons of coal per year passing through new facilities at Prince Rupert. Another important move was the agreement, subject to official approval, to take over the Chicago, Milwaukee, St Paul and Pacific Railroad, expected to become effective in 1985. This will add a considerable new network in the northeastern United States to the existing US subsidiaries, administered by the Grand Trunk Corporation. The Grand Trunk's existing components are the Grand Trunk Western and its subsidiary, the Detroit, Toledo and Ironton Railroad; the Duluth Winnipeg and Pacific Railway, and the Central Vermont Railway.

In Canada itself, meanwhile, the decision to bring the rates for grain haulage into line with actual costs by the early 1990s, with government subsidies covering the shortfall in the meantime, should enable Canadian National to increase the pace of track modernization and other capital investment. One of the most important of current projects is the track doubling already under way on the transcontinental main line between Edmonton and Vancouver. By the end of 1983 CN had inaugurated services on its latest stretch of double track, and the longest so far completed, over the 89 miles between Henry House, east of Jasper, and Valemount, to the west of Redpass Junction, where the Prince Rupert branch turns northwest.

Further west, however, where railway officials have predicted the need for three tracks over the 250 miles between Vancouver and Kamloops by 1996, and a fourth by 2020, there are likely to be problems along the Fraser River valley, where CN and CP tracks follow opposite banks. Excavating a wider shelf for the second track and tipping spoil into the river would cause serious obstructions if carried out on both sides, though neither company is in favour of the more obvious alternative of using one of the existing lines exclusively for westbound trains and reserving the other for the eastbound traffic.

CHAPTER FOUR

THE NORTHERN LINES

The main thrust of Canadian railway development was, naturally, along the east-west axis, dictated by the overriding need to link the prairie and Pacific provinces with the original eastern settlements and the requirement for ocean outlets for the products of the interior. As the inland population grew, however, and as the frontiers of agriculture and mineral exploitation moved north, so the railways followed. Usually they received Dominion or provincial government backing, and in some cases have been absorbed into the national system.

One which has remained an independent concern was started in 1899, building north from the new industrial center at Sault Ste Marie. The Algoma Central Railway became the Algoma Central and Hudson Bay Railway in 1901, though the discovery of the iron ore deposits that formed the basis for the Helen mine near Michipicoten Harbour on Lake Superior provided a more immediate target, and in the event the railway never progressed beyond Hearst, on the former National Transcontinental line, reverting to its original name in 1965. The railway was incorporated by Francis H. Clergue, whose exploitation of the hydro-electric potential

of the Sault Ste Marie rapids was the foundation of local industries, and construction started both inland from Michipicoten and north from Sault Ste Marie. The work was halted in 1903, with the grading completed between the two starting points but only 84 miles of track laid, as a result of the collapse of Clergue's enterprises, but provincial guarantees allowed the work to be continued. By the end of 1912 the main line had reached a junction with the Canadian Pacific at Franz, with a branch from Hawk Junction to Michipicoten. Beyond Franz the line was continued to a junction with the Canadian Northern at Oba and on to its northern terminus at Hearst. The work involved many difficult stretches, including the descent to the floor of the narrow Agawa Canyon just over 100 miles north of Sault Ste Marie, and the crossing of the muskegs north of Franz, where wooden pilings were used to form floating bridges across the swamps.

The country through which the railway runs is almost entirely unsettled, and it operates primarily as a carrier of mine and forest products and goods manufactured from them. As well as the railway itself, the company has marine, trucking and real

2-8-0 locomotive No 23 was among the early motive power on the Algoma Central Railway, which runs north from Sault Ste Marie to the lumber town of Hearst.

A wood-burning locomotive pushes a mixed train over one of the many trestles that were needed to carry the Algoma Central through the wilderness.

estate divisions. The first of these dates from the end of the 19th century, when materials for the Michipicoten branch were brought to the harbor by barge, and in recent years has come to account for half or more of the company's revenue, produced by a total of 15 vessels operating on the Great Lakes. The forestry business, based on 850,000 acres of land grants, supplies lumber, pulp and paper mills at Hearst and Sault Ste Marie, and forest products currently account for around 14 percent by weight of total rail freight. Traffic provided by mining has declined over the last 10 years from about 65 to 55 percent of the annual total, manufactured goods accounting for the remainder.

Total traffic in the period 1973–82 averaged 3,700,000 tons, though the effects of the recession were evident in the 1982 total of only 2,235,000 tons, the lowest since 1945. Nevertheless, the company remains profitable – a relatively recent state of affairs, only achieved in the years since 1952, when the Algoma Central became the first Canadian railway to complete the conversion to diesel traction. Current equipment includes nine road, 22 road switcher and two switcher locomotives and more than 1,400 revenue freight cars, as well as 50 cars used on the regular passenger services and the thriving tourist excursion business.

Another Ontario railway started around the same time, and one which ultimately did reach Hudson Bay, had somewhat different origins. In 1900, in response to the demands

of settlers in the region to the north of Lake Temiskaming, the provincial government of Ontario provided $40,000 for surveys of possible rail routes north from the Canadian Pacific's original terminus at North Bay, and two years later work was started on the Temiskaming and Northern Ontario Railway. By 1908 the line had reached a connection with the National Transcontinental at Cochrane, a total of 254 miles, but in the meantime the original purpose of the railway had been overshadowed by the discovery of massive silver deposits at Cobalt. These came to light in 1903, when the railway builders uncovered slabs of almost pure silver ore, so that even before its completion the line had become the focus for extensive mine traffic. Subsequent exploration revealed an abundance of gold, copper, zinc and other ores in the region, and branches were built to such locations as Elk Lake, Timmins and Noranda, Quebec, the last reached by means of the charter of the Nipissing Central Railway, acquired in 1911.

The growth of the mining industry was dependent on hydro-electric power, and in 1922 the main line was extended some 44 miles beyond Cochrane to a new water power plant at Island Falls on the Abitibi River, followed by a further extension to another plant at Fraserdale. The final northward extension, to Moosonee on James Bay, was completed in 1932, principally as an unemployment relief measure during the great depression. In 1945 the railway's name was changed to Ontario Northland Railway, in order to avoid confusion between its initials and those of the older Texas and New Orleans Railroad. It remains in provincial ownership, and as a result of the early mineral strikes has continued to be profitable from its inception. The conversion from steam to diesel was completed in 1957, and passenger services continue to operate alongside the principal business of freight transport.

Only one other railway has a terminus on Hudson Bay. Now part of Canadian National, the Hudson Bay Railway took even longer than the Ontario Northland to complete, and had a much more complex history. The first charters for railways to the bay were granted in 1880, and within two years no fewer than nine companies had been formed for the purpose, though the only serious attempt was made by the Winnipeg and Hudson Bay Railway and Steamship Company, one of the two original charters. With the promise of federal subsidies of 6,400 acres of land per mile of track, and backed by provincial bond guaran-

tees, the line was built 40 miles to Shoal Lake in 1886. Delays in the settlement of land grant claims were followed by complex political maneuvring, whose ultimate result was the eclipse of the Hudson Bay project by Mackenzie and Mann's Lake Manitoba Railway and Canal Company. The latter was built as far as Dauphin, to the west of Lake Manitoba, by the end of 1896, but this was indicative of the generally western and northwestern trend of the future Canadian Northern Railway.

The Hudson Bay route continued to be a political issue. The prairie provinces, after the creation of Saskatchewan and Alberta in 1904, demanded their own ocean outlet via the bay, but the federal government was reluctant to pay for such a dubious enterprise. Mackenzie and Mann were prepared to build as far as The Pas for the land grants involved, but their terms for continuing to the bay were designed to compensate them handsomely for their trouble; by 1910, when the line to The Pas was opened, government surveys had

Autumn foliage forms a spectacularly colourful backdrop to a diesel-hauled passenger train on the Algoma Central.

Facing page, top: The Algoma Central Railway's Snow Train excursion heads through the Agawa Canyon, during the months when the grip of winter transforms wilderness into wonderland.

An Algoma Central passenger train on the 1,550ft long, 130ft high curving trestle that carries the line over the Montreal River 92 miles north of Sault Ste Marie.

Cars of an Algoma Central excursion train at rest in the wilderness park developed for visitors to the Agawa Canyon, 114 miles north of Sault Ste Marie.

Algoma Central train and autumnal scenery are reflected in the waters of Trout Lake, where old Forest Ranger buildings have been converted into summer cottages.

101

located alternative routes to Churchill and Port Nelson, but the only contract placed was for a bridge over the Saskatchewan River at The Pas. In the elections of 1911 the Conservatives made good use of the Liberal government's delays, adopting the Hudson Bay railway as a prominent part of their campaign in the prairies and regaining power, whereupon construction was begun toward Port Nelson.

By the end of 1913, with the roadbed almost complete, just over 100 miles of track had been laid, but shortages of labor and materials resulted from the outbreak of war in the following year and gradually slowed the work. It stopped in 1917, with 333 miles of track laid as far as Kettle Rapids, 90 miles short of Port Nelson, where substantial work had been done on port installations. In 1919 Canadian Government Railways took over the line, initiating services over the first 214 miles from The Pas, and in 1922 the gov-

Below: On the Algoma Central's Smoky subdivision, north of Franz, wooden pilings were used to support the track on floating trestles across the muskegs.

ernment decided to remove the remainder of the rails. Once again political controversy flared, with the result that in 1926 it was decided to complete the line to Churchill, which offered a natural harbor and savings on port construction that would more than offset the expense of the longer railway. Finally, in the spring of 1929, after considerable upgrading of the existing line and with the addition of 175 miles of new construction, the railway reached Churchill; in 1932 regular shipments of grain began.

As a grain export route, the Hudson Bay railway always had more political than practical significance: it gave the prairies their own ocean port, but it could be used for only three months of the year and involved a sea passage, which attracted very high insurance rates. However, the subsequent development of mineral discoveries has conferred greater importance. In the 1950s, as well as a line due north to Lynn Lake, with

branches to Flin Flon and Osborne Lake, a branch was built from the original main line at Sipiwesk, 31 miles north to the nickel mines around Thompson.

Provincial support was also responsible for another prairie system, based on a group of independent lines in northern Alberta and taking its name from this location. The originator of this system was J. D. McArthur, who in 1907 incorporated the Edmonton,

Dunvegan and British Columbia Railway, intended to build northwest from Edmonton to Fort George, British Columbia. In the event, the line stopped at Spirit River after 358 miles, with a branch running 139 miles south from Rycroft to Grande Prairie; the line was opened as far as McLennan in the spring of 1915, and to Spirit River and Grande Prairie in July of the following year. Meanwhile, McArthur had acquired the charter

Above: Scene on the Edmonton, Dunvegan and British Columbia Railway, now the Northern Alberta Railways Grande Prairie subdivision, near Esher in 1920.

Above: Horse-drawn wagons carry fill for the Sturgeon Bridge, Northern Alberta Railways Edmonton sub-division, during construction work in 1932.

Locomotive No 29 of the Alberta and Great Waterways Railway, one of the lines consolidated into the Northern Alberta Railways in 1929.

of the incomplete Alberta and Great Waterways Railway, and in July 1916 this line was opened between Carbondale, 14 miles north of Edmonton, and Lac La Biche, 114 miles to the northeast. Another six months saw the opening of a third McArthur railway, the Canada Central, for 49 miles between Winagami Junction and the town of Peace River, but at this point the effects of the war forced a halt to construction, and in 1920 all three railways were taken over by the provincial government.

Until 1926, when the province assumed operational control of all three lines, the Grande Prairie and Peace River routes were operated by Canadian Pacific, but in 1928 it was arranged that a new company, Northern Alberta Railways, would be established under the joint ownership of Canadian Pacific and Canadian National. The new company came into existence in January 1929 and the arrangement was continued for 52 years until January 1981, when the system became the Peace River Division of CN.

Under provincial ownership during the 1920s several extensions were made to the original system. By November 1925 the old Alberta and Great Waterways line was extended 173 miles beyond Lac La Biche to Waterways on the Athabasca River, the beginning of the water route via the Great Slave Lake and Mackenzie River to the Arctic Ocean, and close to the industrial centre of Fort McMurray. In November 1927 the Pembina Valley Railway opened a 26½-mile branch line from Busby, 35 miles north of Edmonton, to Barrhead. The end of 1930 saw the completion of 65 miles of new track from Peace River to Hines Creek and by the beginning of 1931 the Grande Prairie line had been

extended 89 miles by way of Wembley and Hythe, in order to reach Dawson Creek in British Columbia.

Early traffic on the Northern Alberta system was produced by the spreading agricultural settlements, but during the Second World War there was a dramatic increase in freight and personnel associated with the Alaska Highway construction. The high level of traffic was sustained until the 1950s, when new roads and the completion of the Pacific Great Eastern Railway to Dawson Creek provided competing outlets, resulting in the curtailment of passenger services – only a twice-weekly service between Edmonton and Fort McMurray is currently provided

An old donkey engine used at Pine Point on the Great Slave Lake Railway, financed by the federal government in the 1960s to provide access to lead-zinc ores.

– and accompanied by a conversion to diesel traction toward the end of the decade. Subsequent mineral developments, notably the construction of the Great Slave Lake Railway in the early 1960s, and the exploitation of oil sands near Fort McMurray, provided new traffic. As a result, the railway continued its program of upgrading track and roadbed, opening new yards at Dunvegan in 1965 and extending its communications facilities to include microwave and VHF radio networks. The latter enables all trains to be in radio contact with the headquarters at Dunvegan.

The Pacific Great Eastern's arrival at Dawson Creek was only one stage in the construction of the biggest of all the provincial railways, and the third biggest in the country, though in its early years it seemed that the venture was doomed never to go anywhere at all. Work started in 1907 from Squamish, 40 miles north of Vancouver, on the Howe Sound, Pemberton Valley and Northern Railway, but only a few miles had been built when the project was turned over

to the provincial government. Little further work was carried out until after the First World War, when it was extended to Quesnel, a total of 344 miles, but with no connection to any other railway it remained a purely local line, serving the thinly-scattered communities of the region.

After the Second World War, however, the province grew ambitious to develop the natural resources of its northwest, and in 1949 a start was made on upgrading the line and extending it to Prince George and a connection with the Canadian National. This was achieved in 1952, and by 1956 a line had been built round the foot of the cliffs between Squamish and North Vancouver, where the railway now has connections with Canadian National, CP Rail, Burlington Northern and the BC Hydro Railway. In 1958 the 197-mile extension to Chetwynd, along with branches of 69 miles to Fort St John and 61 miles to Dawson Creek, brought the railway across the Rockies to the Peace River country. During the 1960s more branches were

Final alignment of newly laid rails on the Manning subdivision of the Great Slave Lake Railway during construction of this ore-carrying line in the early 1960s.

Below: Alongside its main task of carrying lumber and coal to the Pacific ports, the British Columbia Railway runs a passenger service to Prince George.

built, one of 23 miles from Kennedy to the new logging and industrial centre of Mackenzie, and another of 78 miles northwest from Odell to Fort St James. Beyond Fort St John the line was extended 250 miles to Fort Nelson by 1971, but construction of the 412-mile extension from Fort St James to Dease Lake was suspended in 1977 after 147½ miles had been completed.

The railway's newest extension is the Tumbler Ridge branch, part of the province's $2.6 billion development of the northwest coalfield. Investment in the railway alone accounts for some $500 million, and the new

80-mile branch from Anzac was scheduled for completion at the end of 1983. The British Columbia Railway will be responsible for hauling 13,000-ton unit trains of 98 cars each from the mining area to Prince George, where Canadian National will take over for the journey to new port facilities at Prince Rupert. On the Tumbler Ridge line the trains will be hauled by a total of seven GF6C diesel locomotives supplied by the Electro-Motive Division of General Motors. Electrification was selected largely because two long tunnels on the line – one of 5.6 miles and one of 3.79 miles – would require extensive ventilation

Royal Hudson-hauled
excursion on the original
Pacific Great Eastern line
between North Vancouver
and Squamish that formed
the basis for the present-day
BCR.

costing $15 million for diesel locomotives, and to minimise the number of power sub-stations a 50 kilovolt supply is used. The locomotives deliver a diesel equivalent of 6,000 hp, and the nine trains are scheduled to operate on a 75-hour cycle to deliver 10 million tons of coal a year for shipment to Japan from the new terminal at Ridley Island, Prince Rupert.

The new coal contract, which may well be increased in the future, will more than double the railway's freight movements, which hitherto have derived almost entirely from forest products. Expansion of the logging, pulp, paper and woodchip industries is also continuing, and a total of 126 diesel locomotives and nearly 10,000 freight cars continue in service, half of the locomotives and well over half of the cars having been acquired since 1972. Along with this modernization of its rolling stock, the British Columbia Railway has pioneered many ad-

vanced operating techniques such as radio control of mid-train locomotives, and one of its latest innovations involves the installation of visual display units in locomotive cabs. The Location, Identification and Control system of which the VDUs form part also uses transponders between the rails to communicate train movements via the railway's existing microwave radio network to the new headquarters in North Vancouver. Trains are constantly monitored and the speed and location of individual trains, along with operating instructions from the dispatcher, are transmitted and displayed on the cab VDU.

As a provincial railway, the British Columbia is limited in its scope for further expansion by the provincial boundaries. Possible routes have been surveyed north of Fort Nelson to Nelson Forks, and beyond Dease Lake, and in the early 1970s active consideration was being given to the question of how the latter might be extended across the Yukon boundary to Watson Lake. In the meantime, only one railway has penetrated the Yukon Territory, reaching from Skagway, Alaska, to the territorial capital of Whitehorse. The Whitepass and Yukon Route was originally built at the end of the last century in response to the Klondike gold rush, when Skagway was the principal departure point for prospectors arriving there by sea to begin the daunting climb up the Chilkoot Pass to the Yukon River. The railway was built in just over two years, starting in April 1898, and in view of the difficulties of the terrain used a 3ft gauge. Even so, the final cost of some $10 million reflected the employment of as many as 35,000 construction workers.

The railway survived the end of the gold rush and during the Second World War was taken over by the US Army for Alaska Highway traffic. Following the war the company was reorganized, the White Pass and Yukon Corporation including the Pacific and Arctic Railway and Navigation Company, the British Columbia-Yukon Railway Company, the British Yukon Railway Company and the British Yukon Navigation Company. Their names reflect the international nature of the route – from US territory in Alaska, across the corner of the province of British Columbia into the Yukon Territory – and the British capital used for its construction. Subsequently, the track was rehabilitated and an efficient and profitable transport operation was developed, the company operating extensive trucking services in conjunction with an integrated rail-ship container system for lead-zinc concentrates.

Unfortunately, three-quarters of the railway's traffic was provided by the Cyprus Anvil lead-zinc mine, which closed in 1982. As a result, the railway itself suspended operations indefinitely in October 1982. In its last full year of operation the railway had carried 555,323 tons of freight but only 374 passengers, and there seemed little prospect of its reopening after a year of closure.

The original Pacific Great
Eastern line alongside Howe
Sound plays host to an
excursion hauled by a
former Canadian Pacific
Royal Hudson.

CHAPTER FIVE

RESOURCES RAILWAYS

Previous page: The sole purpose of the Cartier Railway in northern Quebec is to carry iron ore from the mines of the interior to Port Cartier on the St Lawrence.

In the sense that Canada's main asset at Confederation was the vast tract of unsettled land in the west, and that railways have always depended on the traffic generated by the exploitation of natural resources, all Canadian railways can be considered as resources railways. However, alongside the lines that have developed on traditional patterns, providing a means of transport for whatever an area might produce, there have been others built for a single, specific purpose, either as public enterprises or as part of a private company's activities. Among these lines are some of the oldest and some of the newest, as well as some of the most interesting.

Historically, railways developed out of the tramways built to serve mines, usually to transport their products to a nearby waterway, and one of the earliest steam-operated railways in Canada was just such a line. The Albion Railway was built in the 1830s to replace an older tramway that had served the Pictou coal mines in Nova Scotia. Opened in 1838 with three Hackworth locomotives from England, the Albion Railway was operated until the mines were closed around 1890. One of the locomotives, *Albion*, was exhibited at the World's Fair in Chicago in 1893, and subsequently appeared at the centenary celebrations of the Baltimore and Ohio Railroad before finding a permanent home on display at New Glasgow, Nova Scotia.

Perhaps more typical were the many small railways built to help in logging operations. Often these would be no more than temporary tracks a few miles long, and various types of specialized steam locomotives were developed to work the log trains. The geared-drive Robb type was developed for this purpose at the beginning of the century and was specifically designed to use wooden rails. While such lines were normally adjuncts to the traditional means of transport, being used to carry the felled trees to a river bank, some of the logging railways grew into more substantial enterprises. The Spruce Falls Power and Paper Company's line north from Kapuskasing, for example, was built in 1923 to help with the construction of a hydro-electric plant on the Mattagami River at Smoky Falls. The plant supplies power to the paper mill at Kapuskasing, and the railway continues in use ferrying lumber to the mill, which produces paper for the *New York Times*.

Municipal enterprises have also involved railway construction, as in the case of the Greater Winnipeg Water District Railway. This line was started in 1914 from St Boniface, and ran 102 miles along the route selected for an aqueduct to bring water to the city from Indian Bay on Shoal Lake, part of the Lake of the Woods complex. The railway was originally built specifically to facilitate the construction of the aqueduct, but after completion of the latter in 1919 the railway was operated as an independent concern. In its early years, the bulk of its traffic came from forest products, but more recently gravel

became the main bulk cargo, with mixed passenger and freight trains operated as well.

Another railway which began as an amalgamation of local passenger and freight services has become an important freight-only operation both for local industries and as a link in the CP's unit train route to Roberts Bank. In 1897 the British Columbia Electric Railway became responsible for public transport in the Vancouver area, operating electric street-cars in Vancouver, North Vancouver, New Westminster and Victoria, as well as inter-urban services reaching as far east as Chilliwack. By the early 1950s virtually all the street-cars had been replaced by buses, and the first diesel locomotives had been introduced, but the line to Chilliwack has assumed increasing importance.

An amalgamation of British Columbia utilities in 1962 saw the railway become part of B.C. Hydro, and its current main line, totalling 103 miles from Chilliwack by way of New Westminster and Vancouver to Steveston, includes connections with the Mil-

Below: Mixed freight train on the British Columbia Hydro Railway, successor to the collection of street car and local rail lines around Vancouver.

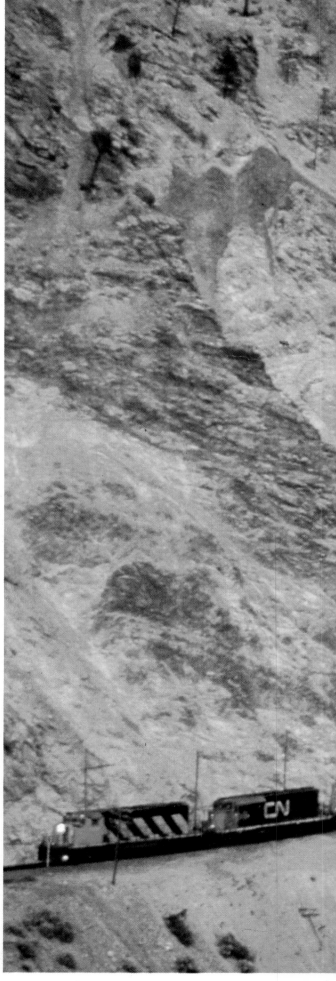

Below: Diesel locomotive on the Roberval and Saguenay aluminium ore-carrying line from Bagotville, on the Saguenay River, to the Arvida smelting plant.

waukee Road and Burlington Northern at Huntingdon and with the British Columbia Harbours Railway, leading to Roberts Bank, at Pratt, as well as with the two national and one provincial railways serving Vancouver. In addition, the CP unit coal trains cross the Fraser River from Mission City on the north bank, running along Canadian National tracks to Livingstone, where the B.C. Hydro provides the connection to Pratt. Much of the B.C. Hydro's own traffic comes from the industrial parks established along its route: from just over $1\frac{1}{2}$ million tons in its first year under its current name, the annual total of freight carried had passed $2\frac{1}{2}$ million tons by the end of the 1970s.

As mineral developments grew in scope, supplementing the original forest-based industries, other railways were built to serve them. The Arvida aluminum smelting plant in Quebec depends on imported ore, and in 1925 a railway was built to ferry bauxite from the port of Bagotville, on the Saguenay River. In a more remote part of the province are two isolated railways whose function is to transport ore from inland mines in both Quebec and Labrador to ports on the St Lawrence estuary. Unlike the Roberval and Saguenay, which connects with the Canadian National line to Quebec City, neither of these lines connects with any other railway.

The first to be built was the Quebec, North Shore and Labrador, whose goal was the vast deposits of iron ore first recorded in the 1890s.

Three Canadian National diesel locomotives head a unit coal train on the tortuous route along the foot of the cliffs in the Fraser River canyon.

In 1949 the Iron Ore Company of Canada was formed to exploit the ore, and in 1950 the first construction equipment was landed at Sept Iles. The construction of the 356-mile line to the new mining centre of Schefferville involved a massive airlift, with new landing strips built to enable men and materials to be flown in, and was completed in February 1954. Within six months the first shipment of ore left the Silver Yard at Schefferville, and almost immediately the company was established as the largest producer of iron ore in Canada. Subsequent mining developments have involved the construction of the 38-mile Northern Land Company railway from a point 224 miles north of Sept Iles to Wabush and Labrador City in the Carol Lake area, where concentrated and pelletised ores are produced. Meanwhile, Labrador City has grown to a population of some 15,000 since its foundation in 1959, and ore shipments from Sept Iles reached a record level of over 27 million tons, the biggest single load being 235,840 tons taken on by the *World Gala* in May 1979.

Ore is ferried to the estuary ports in trains ranging in size from 165 to 260 cars, each carrying almost 100 tons, the journey taking 14 hours from Labrador City and 19 hours from Schefferville. Motive power is provided by a total of 16 1,750 hp GP-9 and 65 3,000 hp SD40 and SD40-2 diesel locomotives, and more than 3,500 ore cars are operated. A particularly interesting aspect of the mining operations is the automated railway that carries ore from the excavations to the crushing plant. Seven trains, each of 20 cars carrying 100 tons each, are in continuous movement between the loading pockets and the crushing plant, where a mechanical dumper lifts two cars at a time to empty the ore into the crusher pits. The whole operation, including the control of the 1,200-equivalent hp electric locomotives, is controlled by electrical signals to servo mechanisms on the trains and switches.

Some 30 miles to the west of Sept Iles is Port Cartier, where US Steel's Cartier Railway has its southern terminus. The Cartier railway was originally opened in 1960, and in 1972 the original 190-mile line to Lac Jeannine was extended 86 miles to Mount Wright where further mining activity was begun. In 1976 the original line added a 3-mile bypass

Three of the Cartier Railway's 54 diesel locomotives at the head of a unit iron ore train bound for Port Cartier on the northern shores of the St Lawrence.

Mid-train locomotive helps power a unit ore train through the winter landscape of northern Quebec as part of the Cartier Railway's year-round operations.

to Fire Lake, following the closure of the original Lac Jeannine excavations. Trains of up to 150 cars are operated, the average weight of ore per train being 12,500 tons, and 54 locomotives along with over 2,000 ore cars are in service on the line.

Equally remote are the lead-zinc ores at Pine Point on the shores of the Great Slave Lake. Until the Mackenzie Highway was built in the years after the Second World War, this region was accessible only by air or along the water route formed by the Athabasca and Great Slave Rivers, and so in order to transport the ores the federal government financed the construction of the Great Slave Lake Railway. This runs 377 miles north from Roma, on the Northern Alberta Railway, to Hay River, with a 55-mile branch running west to the mines at Pine Point, and was completed in 1964. In addition to the mine traffic, this line carries grain and lumber produced along its route, as well as north-bound traffic for the expanding oil and gas explorations in the Northwest Territories. Beyond Hay River, freight is transported further north by barge along the Mackenzie River system in order to reach the still more remote settlements on the shores of the Beaufort Sea.

Development of natural resources is also continuing within the province of Alberta, and in the late 1960s the provincial government financed the construction of the Alberta Resources Railway. It was completed in 1969 and runs 233 miles south from Grande Prairie, on the Northern Alberta Railway, to a junction with the Canadian National main line at Swan Landing. The principal traffic on this line is provided by the coking coal mines in the Smoky River district, whose products are destined for export to Japan, as well as new industrial developments inspired by the railway, which is operated as the Grand Cache subdivision of Canadian National.

Facing page: Ore train, with three diesels at the head, on the Iron Ore Company of Canada's Quebec, North Shore and Labrador Railway, built in the early 1950s.

Below: One of the 65 3,600 hp locomotives used to haul iron ore on the QNS&L between Schefferville and Carol Lake and the port of Sept Iles.

Facing page, top: A British Columbia Railway lumber train crosses the Fraser River at Prince George en route to the US border where another railway will take over.

Three Canadian National diesels at the head of a train of loaded flat cars.

A train of Canadian National box cars headed by two diesel locomotives negotiates an apparently perilous route along the foot of a range of towering cliffs.

CHAPTER SIX

PASSENGER TRANSPORT

Early passenger vehicles on Canadian railways, as elsewhere, were based on stage coach bodies, but just as the English locomotives with their rigid wheelbases proved unequal to the twisting courses of light rails, loosely fastened, so the coaches were soon given independent trucks with four or six wheels. By 1860 all but 10 percent of the cars in passenger service were equipped with trucks, the normal pattern of accommodation being rows of seats down either side of a central aisle. Ventilation was provided by windows and roof ventilators, lighting was by oil lamps, and wood stoves at the ends of the coaches were used for heating.

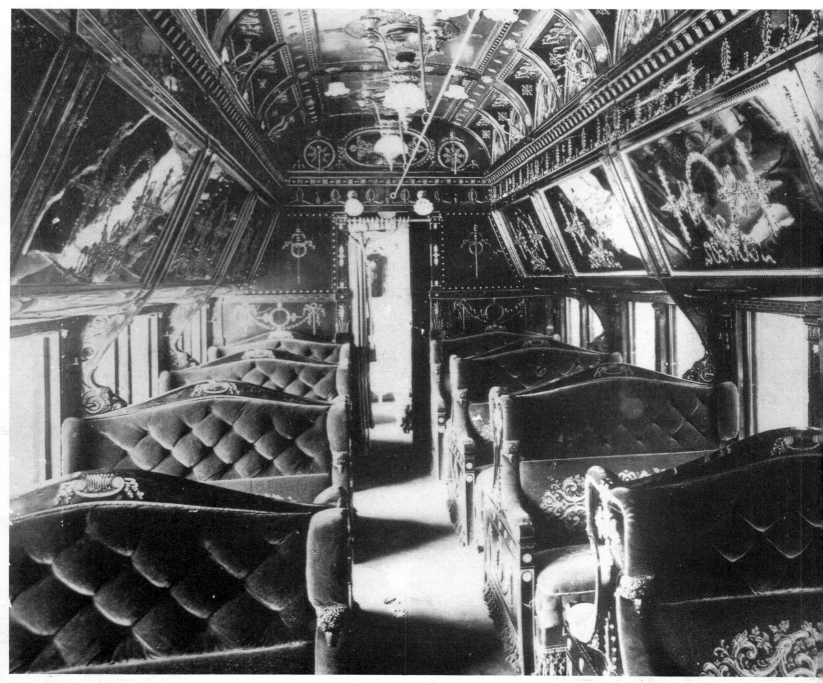

An early innovation was the sleeping car, introduced by the Great Western and Grand Trunk as early as 1857, and by the end of the 1860s the former was operating fairly luxurious sleeping cars with three tiers of berths along either side and drapes for privacy. Perhaps of more fundamental benefit was the introduction of Westinghouse air brakes, automatic couplers and improved operating procedures which helped reduce the alrming number of accidents in the early years. Two particularly bad accidents occurred in 1857 and 1864: the former, in which 60 of the 84 people aboard were killed, occurred when a Great Western train from Toronto crashed through the bridge over the Desjardins Canal on the outskirts of Hamilton. The second disaster, the worst in Canadian railway history, happened on the St Lawrence and Atlantic when a train carrying 350 newly-arrived immigrants plunged into the Richelieu River at Beloeil. The cause on this occasion was the failure of a relief driver to stop before crossing a swing bridge which had been opened to allow a barge to pass, the combination of an unscheduled train and a driver unfamiliar with the line leading to the loss of 100 lives. Taken together, the two incidents pointed to inadequacies in both equipment and procedures, but thanks to subsequent legislation the overall safety record of the railways has been exemplary.

Meanwhile, the completion of the Canadian Pacific line to British Columbia highlighted the need for improved accommodation. The system taken over by the company at its formation included no more than two first class passenger cars and one baggage car, but by the time regular services between Montreal and Vancouver started in 1887 the railway mustered 120 first class, 109 second class and 100 baggage, mail and express cars. The numbers continued to increase at a rate dictated by the volume of traffic, and since the Canadian Pacific's prosperity was directly dependent on the rate at which it could encourage settlement of the prairies, many of the new cars were of the famous colonist pattern. The standard rows of double seats along the sides were of wood and converted into beds for sleeping, while wooden bunks could be lowered from the roof.

First class travel on the Canadian Pacific by the end of the 19th century was a very different matter. The interiors of the cars, whether day coaches for shorter journeys, or the sleeping cars that became standard on longer hauls, were both ornate and luxurious, and service and facilities were of a high standard. This was particularly important for the tourist traffic that formed a significant part of Canadian Pacific's business, and with plentiful land at its disposal the company soon began to build its own hotels at strategic points. The earliest of these hotels was the Chateau Frontenac in Quebec City, soon joined by others in major cities such as Winnipeg, Regina, Calgary, Vancouver and Victoria, and later still Montreal and Toronto, as well as establishments at more remote but outstandingly scenic locations such as Banff Springs and Lake Louise in the Rockies.

4–6–4 Hudson type locomotive No 2842 heads a passenger train out of Montreal's Windsor Station in 1938, when depression was about to give way to war.

To operate the transcontinental trains through the difficult Rocky Mountain section, the Canadian Pacific produced a series of extremely powerful steam locomotives, culminating in the 2–10–4 Selkirks introduced in 1929. These were attached to the trains between Field and Revelstoke, supplementing or taking over from the big Pacifics that hauled the trains over the more level sections. The formation of Canadian National in 1919 had given rise to rival transcontinental services, and during the 1930s both introduced air-conditioned cars, although a scene of more direct competition was on the busy Montreal-Toronto corridor route.

In 1931 Canadian National started a new six-hour service between the two cities. Canadian Pacific, with only a single-track line for more than half the route – whereas its rival's was double-track throughout – responded with a service taking only 15 minutes longer. Both railways used 4–6–4 Hudson type locomotives and, for a few months until the Great Western Railway in England accelerated its Cheltenham Flyer in response, the two trains were the fastest scheduled services in the world. Moreover, the Canadian Pacific run between Montreal West and Smiths Falls, over its double-track section, was the fastest start-to-stop run in the world, 600-ton trains covering the 124 miles in a scheduled time of 109 minutes, which on occasion was reduced to give average speeds of 70 mph. However, the effects of the depression soon put an end to such heroics, and within a couple of years the companies were operating a joint system of pooled trains on the route between the two cities.

Passenger traffic on Canadian railways recovered during the Second World War, reaching a peak of just over 60,000,000 passengers carried in 1944. By 1950 that total had been halved, and in the face of continuing decline the Canadian Pacific turned its atten-

TerraTransport, provides passenger accommodation on local mixed trains. New international services, operated in conjunction with Amtrak, include the International between Toronto and Chicago and the Maple Leaf between Toronto and New York, and VIA Rail also offers a wide range of special-interest package tours. Another innovation, the computerised Reservia system, offering an integrated booking service for hotel, car hire, ferry and airline services, as well as rail and bus journeys, has been accompanied by continuing efforts aimed at providing inter-modal transportation centers in strategic locations.

The most recent figures available for VIA Rail operations show a reduction in the total number of train miles from 15,189,000 in 1980, the first full year in which the corporation was responsible for all trains, to 12,393,000 in 1982. This was largely a result of the 19.5 percent service reductions ordered by the Minister of Transport in 1981 and implemented in stages from November of that year; the consequence in terms of passengers carried was a drop from 8,009,000 in 1981 (up from 7,586,000 in the previous year) to 7,223,000. At the same time, the average journey length declined from 254 miles in 1980 and 242 miles in 1981 to only 218 miles in 1982, so that total passenger miles fell by 18.5 percent from the 1981 figure of 1,936,226,000 to 1,577,439,000 in the following year. Among the services abandoned was the Super Continental, making the Canadian the only remaining transcontinental service.

In return for the reductions in services, VIA Rail was offered an operating subsidy of $1,100 million for three years, plus a capital budget of $460 million. The high level of capital expenditure was necessary to replace obsolete rolling stock inherited from the previous operators. The bulk of new rolling stock has consisted of LRC (Light, Rapid, Comfortable) train sets supplied by Bombardier: delivery of an initial batch of 22 power cars and 50 passenger cars started in July 1981, and the following April the corporation ordered a further 10 power and 50 passenger cars at a cost of $100 million. The LRC trains consist of 3,700 hp diesel locomotives designed to run at speeds of 125 mph on existing track, and separate trailers with automatic body tilt mechanisms

for high-speed operation. The first LRC services covered routes between Quebec City, Montreal, Ottawa, Toronto and Windsor, and the additional trains will be used to extend their use to the maritime provinces and to western routes.

Conventional cars which continue in service with VIA Rail after their transfer from Canadian National and CP Rail include coach, club and sleeper cars. The sleepers offer a variety of accommodation, ranging from private bedrooms for two to single-person roomettes and sections with convertible bunk-seats for day and night use. These are hauled by diesel locomotives, the experiment with turbo-trains initiated by

Canadian National in the 1970s having proved less than satisfactory.

VIA Rail is not the only operator of passenger trains. The Algoma Central, Ontario Northland and British Columbia systems all provide regular passenger services, and the last even has a regular steam train, hauled by a restored Royal Hudson of the Canadian Pacific, between North Vancouver and Squamish during the summer months. Other important aspects of passenger transport are the local commuter trains operated by the Government of Ontario, known as GO-Trains, and the urban transit systems that have spread from Montreal and Toronto to several other Canadian cities. The GO-Trains are

Below: The bi-level cars used on the GO-Transit services allow the number of seats to be increased from the 94 of a standard coach to a more useful 162.

operated by the Toronto Area Transit Operating Authority, and services began in 1967 using new lightweight coaches supplied by Hawker Siddeley Canada. The popularity of the new services was such that demand soon began to outstrip the capacity of the original 94-seat coaches at maximum practical train length and frequency, and the manufacturers, in collaboration with the authority, developed a new design of bi-level coaches, seating a total of 162 passengers.

Before the Second World War, local train services were common in and around Canadian cities. Many of them dated from the 19th century, and generally took the form of light electric railways. In 1925 there were more than 1,700 miles of such lines, but they were rapidly displaced by private automobiles and had all but disappeared 25 years later. Their successors are the metro and light rail networks which have been constructed in recent years as the effects of traffic congestion on inner cities have demanded new alternatives. Toronto was the first city to start building a

metro system, the first section having opened in 1955 with subsequent additions bringing the total route length to 35 miles, with a total of 59 stations on two lines.

Toronto's latest project is a light rail line using the system developed by the Urban Transportation Development Corporation on a 4½-mile line between the suburban center of Scarborough and the end of the existing Bloor-Danforth metro line at Eglinton-Kennedy. The UTDC cars, each of which has room for 30 seated and 55 standing passengers,

use linear motors for improved performance in winter conditions. They are designed to run in pairs under fully automatic control, with rapid braking and acceleration so that a high frequency of service can be maintained. The Toronto line is due to begin operation at the end of 1984, and in the meantime a similar system is being built in Vancouver under the name Advanced Light Rapid Transit. The Vancouver line will run approximately 13 miles between central Vancouver and New Westminster, completing

An elegant new street car for the Montreal Tramways Company poses for the camera in 1944.

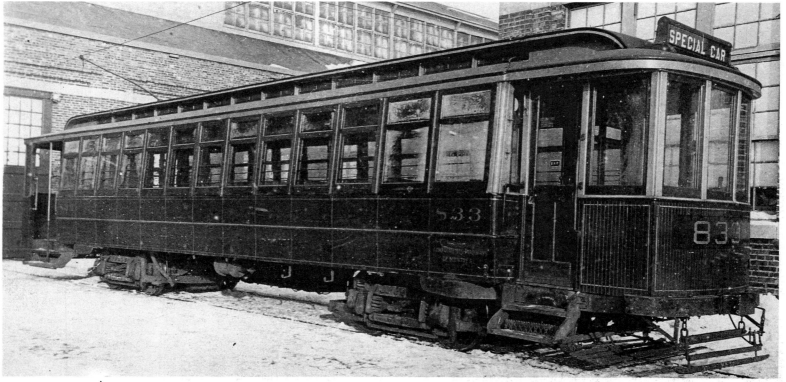

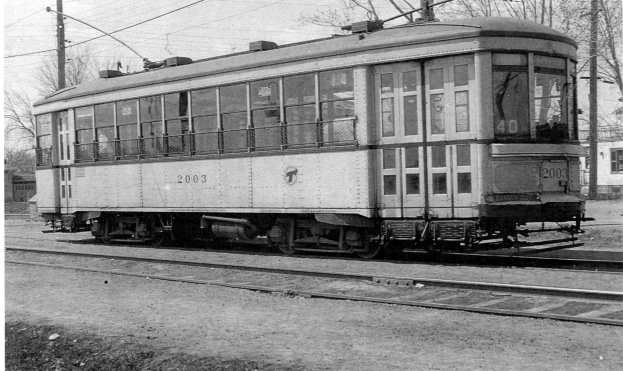

Overhead power lines appeared in many cities as street cars became popular late in the last century: car No 631 of a Montreal street railway in 1900.

Many street railways were built in Canadian cities around the turn of the century: this car operated by the Montreal Tramways Company was photographed in 1907.

A 1929-vintage street car, No 2003, sporting the insignia of the Commission de Transport de la Communauté Urbaine de Montreal.

By 1917, when this car, No 1671, was built for the Montreal street railway, wooden construction and clerestory roofs had given way to more modern styling.

Icicles adorn the sides of street cars in Montreal in the winter of 1944.

the trip in 28 minutes with stops at 13 intermediate stations.

Meanwhile, another metro system was opened in Montreal in 1967, this time using rubber-tired trains of nine cars each. Three lines, with a combined route length of 25 miles and a total of 46 stations, were carrying 150 million passengers per year by 1982, and several extensions were planned or under construction, forming the basis of an extensive rapid transit system. Canada's other two new rapid transit systems are in Alberta, where short light rail lines have been brought into operation in both Edmonton and Calgary. Edmonton's initial $5\frac{1}{2}$-mile line, with six stations, is planned to be joined by a second line of $15\frac{1}{2}$ miles, while two new lines, each of 6 miles, are planned for Calgary, where the original $7\frac{3}{4}$-mile line was opened in May 1981. Both the Calgary and Edmonton systems use cars supplied by Duewag of Federal Germany, operating on a 600 volt DC overhead electrical supply.

A Toronto Transit Commission metro train near Islington station en route to Kennedy station.

Below: Trains on the Yonge Street section of Toronto Transit Commission's Metro system, to the south of Eglinton Street station in June 1976.

One of the fleet of 196 Canadian
Rail vehicles operated by the
Toronto Transit Commission on a
tour of the city.

EGLINTON VIA DOWNTOWN

5046

An example of the early G
Class cars used on the
Toronto Metro, whose first
section was opened in 1955,
when automobiles had
superseded street cars.

The Montreal Metro system.

The first section of
Montreal's Metro was
opened in 1967: here a train
waits at Angrignon to start
the journey to Honoré-
Beaugrand at the other
end of Line 1.

A train set of the Montreal
Metro system's rubber-
tyred cars on a raised track
awaiting maintenance work.

DO NOT ENTER

4005

Servicing some of the rubber-tyred cars used on Montreal's expanding Metro system, the first section of which was opened in 1967.

Pacific Great Eastern Railway 107, 108, *112*, *114*
Pacific Scandal 32
Painsec Junction 26
Palliser, Captain 30, 34
Passenger transport 47–48, *50*, 56, *84*, 89, 99, 107, *110*, 119, 130–149
Peace River 30, 105, 106, 109
Peace River Division 105
Pembina 32
Pembina Valley Railway 106
Penetanguishene 21
Penn-Central 51
Pennsylvania Railroad 51, 82
Phoenix Bridge Company 71–72
Pictou 25
Pictou coal mines 118
Pierce, Jason 9
Pine Point 125
Pine River Pass 30
Pipelines 48
Poor, John 14
Portage La Prairie 24
Portal 42
Port Alberini 42
Port Arthur 37, *66*, 71, 72, 82
Port Borden 27
Port Cartier *118*, 122
Port Huron 19, 73
Portland (Maine) 14, 18, 19
Port Mann 72
Port McNicoll 45
Port Moody 33, 39, 42
Port Nelson 102
Port Simpson 70, 71, 72
Pottinger, David 80
Prescott 13
Prince Albert 45, 66, 67
Prince Edward Island 26, 27
Prince Edward Island Railway 81
Prince George 30, 109, 110, *126*
Prince Rupert 72, 92, 110, 112
Princess Victoria 9

Quebec Bridge 71–72, 73
Quebec (Province) 14, 25, 39, 41, 45, 67, 70, 71, 72, 84, 98, *118*, 120, *122*
Quebec and Richmond Railroad 18
Quebec City 18, 39, 41, 67, 71, 72, 120, 131, 142
Quebec, Montreal, Ottawa and Occidental Railway 39, 41
Quebec, North Shore and Labrador Railway 120, *124*

Rationalisation 42, 48–52, 82
Redpass Junction 84, 92
Red River 30, 32, 37
Regina 45, 131
Reservia system 140
Resources railways 118–125
Richelieu River 9, 131
Richmond 18
Rideau Canal 9
Ridley Island 112
Riel rebellion *36*, 37
Rivers Wilson, Charles 70, 71, 73
Riviere du Loup 26
Roberts Bank 53, 56, 119, 120
Roberval 70, *120*

Rocky Mountains *31*, *32*, 42–45, *60*, 78, 131, 132
Rogers, Major A.B. 33, 34
Rogers Pass 34, 44, 45, 58
Ross, John *16*
Rouses Point 13
Royal Commissions 78–80, 81, 84
Rupert's Land 30
Rutland and Burlington Railroad 13
Rycroft 103

Saguenay River 70, 120
Saint John 14, 25, 42, 47, 56
St Albans *78*
St Boniface 66
St Clair River 19
St Clair Tunnel 73
St John's *6*, 9
St Lawrence and Atlantic Railroad 13, 14, 18, 131
St Lawrence and Ottawa Grand Junction Railroad 13
St Lawrence Bridge 41
St Lawrence Bridge Company 72
St Lawrence River 8, 9, 12, 13, 18, 25, 26, 71, *118*, *122*
St Mary's 19
St Paul and Pacific Railroad 32
St Paul, Minneapolis and Manitoba Railroad 33
Sarnia 15, 18, 19, 73
Saskatchewan 36, *44*, 45, 67, 72, 99
Saskatchewan River 102
Sault Ste Marie 9, 42, 96, 97, 98
Savona's Ferry 33
Schefferville 122, *124*
Schenectady 9
Selkirks 30, 34, *36*
Sept Iles 122, *124*
Shediac 14, 25
Sherbrooke 42
Shoal Lake 99, 118
Sioux Lookout 72
Sleeping cars *20*, *130*, 131, 142
Slocan Lake *22*
Smith, Donald 33, 37, *38*
Smith, Marcus 30
Smoky River 125
Snow Train excursion *100*
Soo Line Railroad 51
South-Eastern Railway 41
Spirit River 103
Spruce Falls Power and Paper Company 118
Spiral tunnels 44–45, *50*, 58
Squamish *96*, 108, 109, *112*, 143
Steam power 48, *86*, *90*, 118, 132–33, 143
Stephen, George *32*, 33, *34*, 37
Stoney Creek bridge *36*, *66*
Stratford 16
Street railways *144*, *146*
Sturgeon Bridge *104*
Sudbury 67, 72
Supercontinental, the *64*, 136, 140
Superior Junction 72
Swan Landing 125
Swan River 67

TerraTransport 89, 140
Tete Jaune *70*
The Pas 99, 102

Thompson River 33
Thornton, Sir Henry 82, *84*
Thunder Bay 30, 52, 56, 66
Timmins 98
Toronto 8, 18, 19, 21, 42, 45, 47, 67, 73, 82, 131, 132, 140, 142, 143, 144–5, *148*, *150*
Toronto Area Transit Operating Authority 142, 144
Toronto, Grey and Bruce Railway 41
Toronto, Hamilton and Buffalo Railway 40, 48, 51, *52*, *56*
Toronto, Simcoe and Lake Huron Union Railroad 21
Toronto, Simcoe and Muskoka Junction Railroad 21
Tourist traffic 131, 140
Trans-Canada Ltd, the *48*
Trans-Canada Railway 70–71
Trois Pistoles 18, 25
Trout Lake *100*
Truro 15, 25, 26, 45
Tumbler Ridge 92, 110
Turbo-trains *136*, 142–3

United States 8, 9, 13, 14, 15, *16*, 19, 30, 32, 34, 42, 66, 73, 82, 92
United States Army 113
Upper Canada 8
Urban Transportation Development Corporation 145
US Steel 122

Valemount 92
Vancouver City *24*, 42, 58, 72, *80*, 92, *96*, *112*, *118*, 120, 131, 135, 143, 145–49
Vancouver's Island 30, 42, 72, 136
van Horne, William Cornelius 34–36, 37
Vermont 13
VIA Rail 56, 89, *130*, 136–143
Victoria 42, 119, 131
Victoria Bridge 18, 73

Wabash 122
Waterloo and Magog Railway 42
Water transport 8–9, 48
Watson Lake 113
Welland Canal 9
Wellington 42
Windsor 15, 18, 42, 45, 142
Winnipeg 30, 32, 33, 34, 37, 42, 45, 66, 70, 71, 72, 131
Winnipeg and Hudson Bay Railway and Steamship Company 99
Winnipeg Osis 66
Wisconsin Central Railway 50–51
Wolf Creek 72
World Gala 122
World War I 80, 82, 105
World War II 47–48, 84, 107, 113, 133

YARD system 52
Yarmouth 45
Yellowhead Pass 30, 33, 70, 72, 78, 84
York 8
Yukon Territory 113

Page numbers in italics refer to illustrations